The Bogus Image of Bernard Shaw

The Bogus Image
of Bernard Shaw

R J Minney

LESLIE FREWIN : LONDON

First published 1969 by Leslie Frewin Publishers Limited,
1 Quebec Street, Marble Arch, London W1

Set in Scotch Roman,
printed by Anchor Press
and bound by William Brendon
both of Tiptree, Essex

09 096280 X

Contents

Introduction

JUST AS A MOUNTAIN, viewed from different angles, provides a series of varied impressions, so must one who has towered above his contemporaries, as Bernard Shaw did, appear differently to those who knew him.

In this book, which is not a biography but a mosaic of impressions of Shaw given to me over the years by H G Wells, Bertrand Russell, Dame Rebecca West, Dame Laura Knight, Dame Sybil Thorndike, Sir Lewis Casson, Sir Cedric Hardwicke, Rex Harrison, Wendy Hiller, Ronald Gow, Greer Garson, Miles Malleson, Constance Cummings, Benn Levy, Henry Andrews, Kingsley Martin, Ivor Brown, Lord Reith, Alan Dent, John Stewart Collis, Maurice Collis, Dame Edith Evans, Arthur Askey, Wee Georgie Wood, Joyce Grenfell, Max Adrian, Ellen Pollock, Feliks Topolski, Canon R J Davies, Mrs Harold Thompson and her daughter Mrs Rosemary Horton, Lord Evans of Hungershall, Mrs Margaret Cole, Mrs Alice Laden (his housekeeper) and others, a number of facets of his personality will be presented which together should provide a truer picture of the real Shaw than would emerge if viewed only from one angle.

In the main there were two distinct and totally opposed images of Shaw – the Public Image and the Private Image. That these two were in no way in accord Shaw was himself fully aware, for when T E Lawrence said to him: 'Your public image is not even a caricature of you. It does not resemble you at all,' he replied: 'I know, I manufactured it myself'; and again, when asked by the Press what he thought of GBS, he replied: 'The most fictitious character I have ever created.'

Why he created this public image is examined here, as is also his attitude to religion, women and sex, money, politics and many other aspects of life, with a close-up of the man in his closing years up to his death in 1950 at the age of ninety-four, when the author talked to him at his deathbed.

RJM

1
Public Image – Private Image

To SAY THAT George Bernard Shaw had two quite distinct personalities is not to suggest that he was in any way a schizophrenic. He was fully aware of the difference and was always able at will to make the transition.

He had, of course, like other highly developed and ceaselessly active intellectuals, many facets, each generated by the moods and the stresses to which events subjected him. But in essence a clear line can separate the two Shaws – the public Shaw, and the real Shaw as he was in private and as his friends saw him. The public image, he confessed, 'I manufactured myself.' T E Lawrence had similarly bisected himself, paraded in Arab garb on public occasions and sought refuge at intervals in secret hiding places and even disguised himself by changing his name to 'Shaw'. He saw through Bernard Shaw's duplicity and told him bluntly that the Shaw the public saw in no way resembled him: it was not remotely a likeness, not even a caricature.

Cursed with an embarrassing shyness from his early youth, Bernard Shaw was in time able to overcome it, but only by a sustained effort spread over many years. Out of this continuing and desperate struggle the public image emerged and he gave to it a flamboyance that his quick brain and his lively wit were able to sustain and to amplify.

Through his long life thousands of examples of this could be noted in the Press. Kingsley Martin, editor of the *New Statesman and Nation*, told me of an occasion when Shaw returned to England after spending Christmas in the West Indies. A large number of reporters met him as he came off the ship. They asked why he had gone away for Christmas. 'Oh,' said Shaw, 'as an Irishman and a Christian, I disapprove of your pagan festivals, and I have to stay out of England at such a time to avoid over-eating and watching other people get disgustingly drunk in order to celebrate a festival which was out of date in the days of Mithras.' This public image, this persona, as Jung would put it, had really nothing to do with the GBS I knew off and on during a period of thirty years.

Linked with his shyness was an oppressive sensitivity. From his earliest years he had come to believe that his family background was exalted. Macduff was thought to have been an ancestor and he was proud that he was descended from a character in one of Shakespeare's plays. His paternal forbears were Scots who had crossed to Ireland towards the close of the seventeenth century. One of them, William Shaw, fought in the Battle of the Boyne in 1690 on the side of William III, the new Dutch King of England. After the victory the young cavalry captain was rewarded, like other officers in the army, with an ample grant of land in the county of Kilkenny. His descendants, blossoming as the new Irish gentry, played a prominent part in the social life of the district; and one of them, Robert Shaw, who founded Shaw's Bank, and amassed considerable wealth, was made a baronet in 1821. His cousin Bernard Shaw, GBS's grandfather, was less fortunate. He left home, married a parson's daughter and had fifteen children, one of whom, George, was the playwright's father. An easy-going man, George accepted an ill-paid clerkship until family influence obtained for him a sinecure in the Dublin Courts of Justice, known as the Four Courts. The office was abolished in 1850 when he was thirty-six and he was lucky to receive a pension – GBS tells us that it was £60 a year; it was in fact only £44 a year. This he sold for £500 and bought a wholesale corn business, which eventually proved to be a failure. Two years later he married, and had three children – two girls and finally, on the 26th July 1856, a son, who was named George Bernard after his father and grandfather.

Of his mother GBS says that she was the 'daughter of a country gentleman, and was brought up with ruthless strictness to be a paragon of all ladylike virtues and accomplishments by her grand-aunt . . . a hump-backed old lady with a pretty face'. It was the aunt's purpose to use her wealth, which was comfortable rather than great, to wipe out – Shaw tells us – an unmentionable stain on her family pedigree; for her grandfather's birth 'was so obscure that there was some doubt as to whether he had any legal parents at all'. He ran a pawn-shop in the name of one of his employees in a poor and sordid quarter of Dublin. With the money this brought he married into a county family, and the hump-backed spinster aunt was resolved that her niece should make a really worthwhile marriage. Lists were prepared of eligible young men and, despite the Shaw family's baronetcy, the impoverished, anchorless thirty-eight-year-old George Shaw was unlikely to be considered even as a runner-up. Not even in desperation would Aunt Ellen have countenanced such a matrimonial venture. Yet the carefully guarded girl, Lucinda Elizabeth Gurly, who had just entered her twenties, readily accepted the proposal of this man who was nearly twice her age. He was impoverished and had a disfiguring squint, which Oscar Wilde's father, the surgeon Sir William Wilde, had merely adjusted to a different angle; his only asset was an exaggerated sense of humour which was all he was able to pass on to his son.

The infuriated aunt immediately cut off her niece: such expectations as George Shaw had of thus supplementing his own meagre income from the corn mill vanished. Why Lucinda Elizabeth accepted him mystified everyone; some thought that the hurried and secret marriage provided the only means of escape from the tyranny of the aged hunchback. Shaw says that his mother was taught to recite two of La Fontaine's fables in French with perfect pronunciation; to play the piano, the wrong way; to sit up straight, speak, dress and behave like a lady – she could have worked as a rag-picker and still have appeared to be 'a species apart from servants and common persons'. But she had 'no notion of the value of money', and could not housekeep on a small income. Nor did she know any of the things that could be left to servants or governesses, solicitors or apothecaries, and so, he adds, 'she abandoned her own children to the most complete anarchy'.

The marriage was not a success. She had been warned that her husband was a drunkard, but this she indignantly refused to believe, for, when she questioned him, he denied it vehemently and declared that he was a life-long teetotaller. She discovered the lie while on honeymoon in Liverpool when, on opening the wardrobe, she found it full of empty bottles. She ran away in horror to the docks to seek employment as a stewardess in a ship that would take her far away from him. But, being molested by some rough dockhands, she returned home again.

Unable to rely on her husband, she decided to make her own way in life. Her son was wrong about his mother's ignorance of the value of money, for, just before going to St Peter's Church to be married, his mother signed a deed transferring the sum of £1,256 9s 2d for trustees to hold for her, thus making sure that her husband would not be able to lay his hands on it; and she was able to supplement the small income from this by giving singing lessons. Some years later her father transferred £1,500 to her 'for her sole and separate use': she couldn't touch the capital, but got the income. The children were left to do what they liked. There was no discipline or guidance either from her or their father. Shaw says of her that she neither hated nor loved anybody. 'The specific maternal passion awoke in her a little for my younger sister, who died at 20; but it did not move her until she lost her, nor then noticeably. She did not concern herself much about us.'

There is a mystery about her relationship with her singing teacher, George Vandaleur Lee, a dark, heavy-jowled, gipsy-like man, who put on successful amateur concerts in Dublin, in which Shaw's mother and elder sister Lucy took part. After a time he and the Shaws set up house together. There were rumours, of course, that Mrs Shaw was living with him; it was even thought that Bernard Shaw might be his son. But there does not appear to be any truth in this: GBS was born three years before the family moved in under the same roof as Lee, though they had lived close enough for this to have happened. The joint establishment was maintained for nine years; then Lee left for London and two weeks later, actually on the twenty-first anniversary of her wedding, Mrs Shaw and the girls went too. GBS, not quite seventeen, stayed on in Dublin with his father.

That Shaw was emotionally affected by all this is obvious. His snobbishness died hard – if it died at all. Again and again in later life he spoke of the disadvantages of belonging to the minor branch of an exalted family. He persuaded himself that his father's drunkenness had led to their being regarded as outcasts. He had also heard unpleasant rumours about his mother and Lee, and may even have wondered what truth there might be in the whispers that he was Lee's son; for he often stressed in his autobiographical writings his remarkable resemblance to his father George Shaw. GBS was furious when his early biographers questioned him about his legitimacy. 'As you describe it,' he wrote to Demetrius O'Bolger, 'my story is one in which the kindly hero, my father, was driven to drink by his wife's infidelity.' And later: 'My mother was one of those women who could act as matron of a cavalry barracks from eighteen to forty and emerge without a stain on her character.' John O'Donovan, writing of 'Shaw and the Charlatan Genius', meaning Lee, says: 'Not one trait that Shaw attributes to his father is reminiscent of himself, and although he assured O'Bolger that he hadn't "one trait even remotely resembling any of Lee's", yet if you string together all the descriptive phrases he applies to Lee you get what is virtually a self-portrait. Heterodox and original . . . a man of mesmeric vitality and force . . . impetuous enterprise and magnetism . . . an active volcano . . . completely sceptical about lawyers and professions generally . . . a fine ear and fastidious taste . . . a moderate liver in all respects . . . interesting . . . always a man apart.' In musical tastes, personal assertiveness, industry, fondness for publicity and general picturesqueness, GBS was much more like Lee than his father, who was easy-going, unassertive and quite futile.

There was one further occurrence in his childhood which he called his 'Shame'. A Protestant by birth and upbringing, he had been attending the Wesleyan Connexional School in Dublin, but 'my parents seem hardly to have considered whether I was educated or not, provided I went to school according to custom'. Lee, who was by now sharing the house with them, decided that a change should be made. Being a Catholic himself, he sent the sensitive twelve-year-old GBS to a Catholic school, the importance of which was socially suspect in a Protestant-ruled Ireland. 'For the son of a Protestant merchant-gentleman,' GBS wrote many years later, 'to associate in any way with its hosts of lower middle-class Catholic children, sons of petty shopkeepers and tradesmen, was inconceivable from the Shaw point of view.' He 'at once lost caste . . . and became a boy with whom no Protestant young gentleman would speak or play'. It was 'so repugnant' to the boy that he could not bring himself to mention it to 'any mortal creature, not even to my wife'. He stayed there for six months and at the end of the term 'flatly refused to go back'. Not until eighty years later was he able to refer to it, and that he did on paper, avoiding even then the gaze of another who

14

might pity him for what he had had to endure all those years ago.

These early psychological scars must be taken into account if one is to understand Shaw's acute sensitivity through his growing years, his shyness, his withdrawal from the company of others, and the creation of a public image behind which he could shelter. He realised early, however, that a scornful finger could pierce through it quite easily if its substance was of thin tissue with nothing to back it. And so he made it his purpose to provide that backing. To his active, acquisitive mind it presented no difficulty. Of music, with which every room of the house echoed incessantly, he had a fairly substantial basis of knowledge; soon it developed into an absorbing passion, which drove him to learn by heart the entire score of some of the greatest operas. To this he soon began to add an understanding and appreciation of another of the arts – the pictures in the National Gallery of Ireland in Dublin. Day after day he toured the rooms studying the paintings with care, and he borrowed books from the public library to supplement his knowledge. This had to be done in such spare time as he had, for at the age of fifteen, while his mother and sisters were still in Dublin, he had to go out to work. He got a job in an estate agents' office at a salary of £18 a year. He told himself that in Ireland at that time an 'estate agency ranked as a profession' – a further indication of his snobbery. He adds: 'Having the introduction of my Uncle Frederick, Chief of the Land Valuation office, without whose goodwill estate agents would have been gravely hampered, I could not engage in manual labour of any kind, and called myself junior clerk.' But in fact, as he admitted later, in his *Sixteen Self Sketches*, he was little more than an errand boy. He had to go out and get lunch for the staff and bought a penny roll for himself. After a year, the cashier having left, he was promoted (such was his industry and skill) to take on the man's work, and his salary was raised to £48 a year. 'I was no longer an

15

office boy. I was chief cashier, head cashier, sole cashier, equal to any of the staff, and the most active and responsible member of it.' That made him feel important: he was somebody at last. An adjustment had been made, impressive to one so young who had unquestionably suffered as a result of his oppressively snobbish awareness of the paternal and maternal strands of inheritance.

In Frank Harris's biography of him, which Shaw not only revised but actually helped to write, appears this revealing passage about GBS's impressionable growing years: 'All through, from his very earliest childhood, he had lived a fictitious life through the exercise of his incessant imagination. . . . It was a secret life: its avowal would have made him ridiculous. It had one oddity. The fictitious Shaw was not a man of family. He had no relatives. He was not only a bastard, like Dunois or Falconbridge, who at least knew who their parents were: he was also a foundling.'

Why did Shaw, who despised his weak, inefficient father, stay with him in Dublin instead of accompanying his mother and sisters to London? Was it because he no longer wished to share the joint *ménage* of his mother with Lee? Actually, Mrs Shaw set up a separate establishment in London: hers was in Victoria Grove (now Netherton Grove) in Kensington, Lee's was in Ebury Street and later in Park Lane. They had quarrelled. Mrs Lucinda Elizabeth Shaw was enraged when Lee abandoned what she called his Method and adopted a speedier way of teaching singing. Shaw tells us that she now regarded him as a charlatan. But what infuriated her even more was that Lee had become sentimental about her elder daughter Lucy, who was eighteen at the time; and he was barred from coming to the house. She set herself up as a teacher of singing, using Lee's old Method, which, Shaw tells us, 'preserved her voice perfectly until her death at over eighty'. It has been thought that Shaw drew on this for *Pygmalion*, in which the pupil, Eliza Doolittle (his

16

mother was known as Elizabeth), speaks more than once (in the Epilogue) of earning her living by using Professor Higgins's method of teaching phonetics. Higgins objected violently and Eliza abandoned the idea. Shaw's mother took a different line. She used it and succeeded, and Lee, she wrote and told her son in Dublin, was ruined. To this, Shaw replied: 'My dear Mother, the same calamity has occurred on an average of three hundred and sixty-five times a year, during my experience of him.'

McNulty, a friend of Shaw's since his schooldays, says that Lizzie Shaw left for London because things had reached a point in the 'unhappy Shaw household' when she and her husband finally decided to separate. Mr Shaw, he adds, brought court proceedings against his wife, citing Lee not as an 'offender against the sacredness of holy matrimony', but as 'an object of jealousy'. No one in Dublin, he goes on to say, believed that Mrs Shaw had any more feelings towards this strange being, Lee, save that of friendship.

After working for four and a half years as a clerk, during which, he says, 'I was not precluded from giving myself certain airs', so that his social standing would appear to be as good as that of 'my associates . . . University men', Shaw decided to leave. He was not quite twenty when he crossed the Irish Sea for London and moved in with his mother. He sacrificed a salary, which was by now £84 a year—that is thirty shillings a week— for a hope that, if not at once then at some time in the future, he would be able to find his feet. Meanwhile his mother would provide him with a bed and something to eat. She did, but she was hardly aware that he was there. She went on teaching; pupils kept coming in, most of them women; the elder daughter Lucy was appearing in musical plays on the stage; Agnes, the younger girl, had by now died of tuberculosis.

Shaw tried to make a living as a writer, and failed. 'I had one article accepted. It brought me fifteen shillings.' He wrote some verses to go with a few old picture blocks a firm of publishers wanted to use up and was paid five shillings for it. His clothes got shabbier and shabbier; he was ashamed to go out in them. Not having money for cabs or buses, he had to walk. It was a most embarrassing situation, and he spared himself the indignity of making friends in such circumstances. A public image was impossible to sustain – there was no public.

As it happened, Lee came to his rescue. He was always fond of the boy and took the keenest interest in helping him during his growing years. A number of letters from Lee to Shaw during the nine years 1877 to 1886 still survive and are preserved in the British Museum. They show that Lee tried to get work for the forlorn, penniless, young man as a writer on the staff of one of the musical papers. In this he was unsuccessful; but, on being asked by the Editor of *The Hornet* to act as music critic himself, Lee got Shaw to 'ghost' the articles for him. It is not clear whether Lee passed on the entire sum he received or only a part of it; but we know that between the 29th November 1876 (that is to say, six months after Shaw's arrival in London) and the 28th March 1877 Shaw wrote eighteen articles for *The Hornet* in Lee's name and was paid a guinea each for them – these brought him a total of eighteen guineas in four months. He also acted as Lee's press agent (although Lee was in a sense his mother's rival as a teacher of singing) and was paid various small sums for general expenses. Lee wrote to him: 'Your MS and corrections are admirable – my proof will be returned to you. The enclosed' – Shaw indicates in red ink that it was £5 – 'is to pay for subscriptions to libraries and books that you may require to work on the result that will regenerate the musical world. When more coin is wanted I shall be glad to send it. Hope to see you soon for a chat.' Lee also engaged Shaw occasionally as accompanist on the piano during his singing lessons. '20th March '83 – would you accept a guinea for four visits a week to Mrs Bell to try over her songs – at any time that would suit you, an hour each?' And Shaw was given the tiny part of the Solicitor in Lee's production of Gilbert and Sullivan's light opera *Patience*.

All this ceased when Lee died in 1886 at the age of fifty-five. Shaw tells us that in his last years Lee was very hard-up.

His own struggles in London were not unexpected; he was young, untrained for a career and without any financial reserves; but he was optimistic and energetic enough to feel that the phase would be transient. He walked the streets in broken boots and a pair of trousers with holes worn in the seat, which he relied on the tails of his faded frock-coat to hide. The edges of the cuffs were trimmed with scissors and his tall hat was 'so limp with age that I had to wear it back-to-front to enable me to take it off without doubling up the brim'. He tried to live on sixpence a day. Work of a sort could have been found. He could have gone back to clerking or being a cashier, but that, he doubtless felt, would involve a return to a humbler social status which he hoped he had left behind him for ever.

But something had to be done. He decided to write. Writing had a certain dignity, whether one succeeded or not. He was aware of this. 'My main reason for adopting literature as a profession was that, as the author is never seen by his clients, he need not dress respectably. As a stockbroker, a doctor, or a man of business, I should have had to wear starched linen and a tall hat, and to give up the use of my knees and elbows. Literature is the only genteel profession that has no livery – for even your painter meets his sitters face to face – and so I chose literature.'

Ghosting for Lee had doubtless shown him that he could juggle skilfully with words and he soon saw that his words assumed a startling brilliance, lighting up the skies with an arresting glow; and he had, too, an engaging sense of humour, much richer and more ebullient than his father's. A wide canvas was needed to provide considerable scope; and so he set out to write a novel.

19

He was still busy on odd jobs when he embarked on the writing of *Immaturity* in March 1879, three years after his arrival in London. He was twenty-three years old then. Though a massive book, he finished it in nine months and sent it off hopefully to one publisher after another, but all of them rejected it.

It was a sad blow, for Shaw had slaved for long, exhausting hours, but so great was his faith in his own ability that he confidently started writing his next book, again a novel, which he hoped would fare better and bring him financial independence. It didn't. Like the first, this was rejected too, and so were the third and the fourth and the fifth. His efforts, spread out unremittingly over five years, remained unrewarded. Despite his brave persistence, there must have crept into his thoughts, increasingly as each rejection followed the others, if not a loss of faith in his own ability, then certainly a sense of humiliation. What had happened to the public image he had been trying to sustain but could not with his clothes so shabby and his pockets empty? Shaw tells us that in those first nine years in London, from 1876 to 1885, he earned only £6. He was wrong: the money Lee helped him to get totalled rather more than that. But the time had come for him to make an adjustment. So in 1885 he gave up novel writing. The rejected manuscripts were put away in drawers. He decided to branch out on a fresh line.

His appearance was not at that time attractive. Very tall, painfully thin and bony, a head of bright red hair and a meagre red beard, his face a pallid white, only his eyes held one's attention, if one saw them, for most of the time he was hurrying through the streets with long strides going to the National Gallery and the Reading-Room of the British Museum and occasionally, when he had a shilling to spare, to a concert or to the theatre. The books he read at that time were mostly on good behaviour – a not surprising choice as he was still striving to be a gentleman, to attain the distinction and polish that he regarded as his rightful heritage of which circumstances had cheated him.

'I was a provincial,' he writes, surveying his humiliation during those years and his undimmed faith and bouyancy. 'I was opinionated; I had to change London's mind to gain my sort of acceptance or toleration.' And that was when the biggest build-up of his public image began. It was a build-up of attitude – a startling reversal of every opinion that was widely accepted – a resolve to attract attention, to make himself the focal point of intellectual discussion and even controversy. That, he decided, was the path to acceptance, and he pursued it carefully, painstakingly – it took time, but in the end he achieved his goal.

A vital step in this adjustment was his discovery, at the British Museum, of a French translation of Karl Marx's famous book *Das Kapital,* on which the Communist creed was based. Marx had died two years earlier and there was no English translation of the book. Shaw made a close study of it and instantly became a convert. But what was more important at that juncture was that he met at the museum a journalist named William Archer who was a dramatic critic on a magazine called *The World.* Archer got him a job as art critic on that publication and also the opportunity to review books for a London evening newspaper called the *Pall Mall Gazette.* Shaw's career had begun as a writer. In that first year he earned £117.

The influence on him of Karl Marx's book was much more than political. For Shaw it opened a completely new line of thought and he felt that the only way in which he could achieve a break-through in his career as a writer would be by abandoning the well-trodden paths and beating out a fresh track for himself. This became apparent in everything he wrote, and later in everything he said. His articles on art, his reviews of books, his criticism of music, and his attitude to the theatre were a complete departure from the accepted approach of all other

21

writers. His every pronouncement was the complete reversal of the hallowed, authoritative judgments of the experts. Despite the contempt and scorn poured upon him, this practice was never abandoned, but was most vigorously maintained in his public speeches and was eventually introduced into all his plays; for he saw that the widespread denunciation brought him immense publicity and the name of Bernard Shaw, though often uttered with a sneer, came to be well known. And so, while thus standing on his head, he challenged every windmill, wearing the cap-and-bells and using the clown's ridiculous bladder to drive home his argument. It was not the boy who stood on the burning deck: he had to establish that the deck stood on the burning boy. The public laughed at the performance and soon many began to feel that there was some truth in his bluster. He appealed in the main to the young thinkers and to all who were dissatisfied with the existing standards (as many are in every generation).

Asked in the fulness of his success what he thought of Bernard Shaw, unhesitatingly Shaw replied: 'My greatest work of fiction.' It was, but there was a solid and admirable backing of brilliance to support it. In time his actual achievement took him so far ahead of the public image he had created that he no longer needed it; yet he kept on tinkering with it, expanding and inflating it right up to the end of his long life.

Was he very different away from this – in his home, with his friends, with his servants? I found him so. T E Lawrence and Kingsley Martin, whom I have already quoted, also saw the very marked difference. Dame Sybil Thorndike, who knew him for more than forty years, told me: 'In public he was a know-all and tried to appear to be so; in private he behaved like an ordinary person: there were things which he admitted he didn't know and had tried to understand. He didn't dogmatise. He was conscious of his own shortcomings and there was at times a humility about him. He was amusing, of course –

always most amusing. There was a laugh in his eyes and a laugh in his voice.'

Joyce Grenfell, who knew him when she was a child and also saw him later in life, noticed the difference too. 'He was very kind and attentive to young people,' she told me. 'He once gave me six photographs of himself and said: "One for every day of the week and all out on Sunday. And *don't* sell them till I am dead. They'll be more valuable then."

'A few years later when I was thinking of becoming a commercial artist, he kindly looked at some drawings. "What you need," he said, "is a good agent or a Jewish grandmother. Everyone ought to have a Jewish grandmother" – the implication was that if one had a Jewish grandmother one wouldn't need an agent.

'When I was much older and was able to notice his behaviour towards grown-ups, I found him quite natural; but from time to time his public image used to break in when he talked and the showing-off returned. It had become a part of him and he could not drop it completely.

'Mrs Shaw used to listen to his exaggerations with an amused smile, but once when he was launched on an extravagant account of Mrs Patrick Campbell's beauty, talent and charms, Mrs Shaw, who was then over eighty, showed a little flash of feminine pique and was heard to murmur: "Nonsense, GBS. Nonsense!" She was sitting outside his immediate circle that afternoon, knitting by the window, and I thought then what an attractive and intelligent woman she was.'

The poignancy of Mrs Shaw remembering at the close of her life her husband's mad infatuation for Mrs Patrick Campbell will be the more understandable on reading a description of that association in a later chapter.

2
The Philanderer

ACTUATED BY THE normal urges of adolescence, Shaw appears not to have indulged in even innocent flirtations until he had passed his middle twenties. He told Frank Harris, the editor of *The Saturday Review*: 'I had been perfectly continent except for the involuntary incontinences of dreamland, which were very infrequent.' True he had neither the money to take girls out, nor the clothes; and when he did begin his philandering at the relatively mature age of twenty-six, he confined his attentions to the women who came to the house to take singing lessons from his mother.

The first of these was Alice Lockett, a hospital nurse who was also a Sunday-school teacher. The only outlet his passion found was in love-letters and some flat and uninspired poems, of which this verse, with a playful alteration of her name, is an example:

> *Love lifted to his lips a chalice*
> *And said, 'My power though many mock it*
> *Hath triumphed over the charms of Alice.*
> *Here's to the health of Alice Sprockett'.*

His letters to her went on for two years; of these about twenty still survive. That was the form most of his love-making was to take: he used to sit up far into the night writing extravagantly of his consuming devotion to each of the women in turn. Today he would have been described as a 'Paper Lover'. Was he in love with them – or was it an exercise in love-letter writing to see whether

24

he could make his words win hearts? That it pandered also to his vanity is obvious: in the building up of his ego it helped to reassure him that, whatever his other failings, he did not lack the ability to arouse a romantic response in women.

These early letters betray a very youthful attempt at wooing. He was unsure of himself. Again and again he asks for forgiveness: if he has said anything to hurt or embarrass her it was unintentional; and, having said that, he then goes on to assert that he really means the things he said. 'There. Is it not outrageous? Burn it. Do not read it. Alas! It is too late. You have read it.' There is a great deal of egotism, an analysis of his attitude towards life, an assertion of his righteousness and his conscience – possibly to assure her that he had no designs on her virginity (his own was still intact); and recurrent instances of 'showing off'. All rather childish and foolish: he obviously did not know much about women. He reproaches her for having been severe with him at tea-time; informs her on another occasion that, because of her eagerness to catch a train, he got drenched by the rain and is due for an attack of rheumatic fever. Another letter is signed 'Yours with the most profound Indifference and in the most entire Freedom from any attraction on the part of Any Woman Living – GBS'. He took this back later, saying, 'We are petulant children who should be petted and kissed. I am too big to be petted but you are not too big to be kissed.' Her beautiful complexion, he added, had tempted him often, but, 'Enough. Midnight strikes. My head is in a tumult with matters about which you do not care twopence.' A letter followed with this abrupt ending. After addressing her as 'Dear Miss Lockett', he told her that their acquaintance 'should cease and for ever. When we next meet let it be as strangers. I relinquish our acquaintance, which was never more than the amusement of an idle hour, without regret, save for ever having formed it.'

What had happened we do not know. But it was not

the end. The letters went on. 'Miss Lockett' became 'Dear Alice' and even 'Dearest Alice'. The final surviving letter, which may not have been the last, is dated 8th October 1885. 'Avant, sorceress,' he wrote. 'Love-making grows tedious to me – the emotion has evaporated from it. This is your fault.' It is doubtful that 'love-making' had then the present accepted meaning, and the following passage appears to confirm this: 'I only value friends for what they can give me: if you can only give me one thing I shall value you only for that. It is useless for you to protest – the matter is not within my will – you will be valued as you deserve, not as you wish to be valued. . . . I want as much as I can get.'

He got it in fact from Jenny Patterson, who came into his life at this time. There is no doubt that he had an *affaire* with her; indeed he boasted of it later, even mentioning her name, and explained his long chastity, up to the age of twenty-nine, as being due to his poverty and his natural fastidiousness. It may, of course, be that Shaw was less highly sexed than most normal men, many of whom are equally poor and possibly as fastidious. But it should also be remembered that, hard though he was trying to establish a public image, he was, even while nudging thirty, abnormally shy.

It was Jenny Patterson who helped him to get over it. She was a widow and fifteen years older than him, which makes her age forty-four; she too was one of his mother's pupils and a close friend of both his mother and sister. She was comfortably off and lived in a house in Brompton Square, which even today has lost none of its elegance. Shaw's interest in her was roused as early as February of that year, 1885. There are references to her in his unpublished diary. In April, he records, he had come away early from a concert in order to visit her at her house. In that month his father died at the age of seventy-one. The pound a week he had sent his family as an allowance ceased, but his widow received £100 from the insurance company and she gave her son £11 of it. He went out at once and bought some clothes for himself from Jaeger's – the 'first garments I have had for years'.

By July he was seeing quite a lot of Jenny. On the 4th of that month he stayed with her until 1 am and a few days later, after her lesson with his mother, he walked across the Park with her to her home. He records: 'Supper, music and curious conversation and a declaration of passion. Left 3 am. *Virgo intacta* still.' On the 18th July the diary notes, 'Forced caresses'; and on the 26th, his twenty-ninth birthday, we are told he had 'a new experience', which he elaborated later to 'seduced and raped'; he described her as being 'sexually insatiable' and published a photograph of her in his book *Sixteen Self Sketches* to illustrate a chapter on his sexual experiences. By then Jenny was dead.

The *affaire* with her went on for years. She had an explosive temper and there were many tempestuous scenes between them, some of which he used in his plays while she was still alive. He always insisted that she had pursued him. He liked to portray himself as a non-consenting male ceaselessly pursued by women who were desperately eager to give their consent. 'As soon as I could afford to dress presentably, I became accustomed to women falling in love with me,' he wrote to Frank Harris. 'I did not pursue women: I was pursued by them.' This was not true. Resplendent in his new Jaeger suit, which gave him fresh confidence and courage, and presumably impressed Jenny, he found himself suffering agonies of disappointment from time to time. She put him off one evening to see Lord Croft; on New Year's Eve he went to her house and found the place in darkness. He waited hopefully and listlessly in the Square, listened to the sounds of revelry from the other houses, but hers was silent. Had he made an appointment which she did not keep, or had he stupidly taken a chance in order to surprise her? We do not know. A week later he went again to see her and the single word 'Revulsion' in his diary

27

records his feelings. Three days later he found another man there, who was, Shaw records, 'bent on seduction, and we tried which should outstay the other. Eventually *he* had to go for a train. . . . To bed late.' So all seems to have ended well.

The scenes began shortly afterwards. Enraged possibly on discovering that there were other men in Jenny's life, Shaw began to go out with other women. One of these was May Morris, daughter of the poet, William Morris; another was Annie Besant, a pretty, young intellectual, active as a public speaker and to become one of the outstanding political women of the day, who ended her life battling for the freedom of India. Jenny, who was possessive and jealous, happened to find a letter to him from Annie Besant. She said nothing but decided to spy on them. Seeing them together in a London street, she made an embarrassing scene. Shaw was furious and wrote to say that in future their 'intercourse must be platonic'. This made Jenny hurry round to his mother's house to see him. There was, he records, 'much pathetic kissing and petting after which she went away comparatively happy'. But Shaw refused 'to budge from our new platonic relations', and this caused Jenny to move into the house with him, his mother and his sister; they were now living in Fitzroy Square, near Baker Street. She kept popping up to his room and interrupting his work and, he tells us, he had to play Haydn on the piano in order to steady his nerves. Things got worse. 'JP came, raged, wept, flung a book at my head. . . .' His only escape was to go out into the street and try to write his articles by the inadequate illumination of a street lamp, but Jenny followed him even there.

They were still seeing each other and having scenes five years later, but by then, recording that, 'it looks like breaking off', he took up with another girl, Florence Farr. He was thirty-four years old now and the newcomer was to play the leading role in his first play *Widowers' Houses* a year or two later. Jenny Patterson had gone abroad and Shaw took full advantage of her absence.

But Jenny found out as soon as she got back. He records: 'Fearful scene about FE' – Florence was married to an actor named Emery, who had left her after four years – 'this being our first meeting since her return from the East. Did not get home until 3 am.' The scene was resumed the next day and went on for weeks. One night, on returning from the Opera at Covent Garden, Shaw found Jenny waiting for him outside his house. After placating her, he drove her home in a hansom-cab and walked back, having no money for the return journey. Shaw told Florence about it; being easy-going and good-natured, she took it quite calmly.

Things came to a head two and a half years later on the 4th February 1893. This is what Shaw said about it: 'In the evening I went to FE, and JP burst on us very late in the evening. There was a most shocking scene, JP being violent and using atrocious language. At last I sent FE out of the room, having to restrain JP by force from attacking her. I was two hours getting her out of the house and I did not get her home until near one, nor did I get myself away until three.' Mrs Jenny Patterson was fifty-two years old at this time, Florence more than twenty years her junior. Shaw was thirty-seven. He made Jenny write a letter to him apologising for her frightful behaviour and promising not to annoy Florence again.

The horrible, unforgettable scene was used by Shaw in his play *The Philanderer*. Jenny is portrayed as Julia Craven and Florence as Grace Tranfield. The play was not publicly performed until twelve years later – Shaw could find no market for his plays at that time. Jenny was still alive, and by then aged sixty-four. It is not known whether she saw the play.

Apart from the unpleasantness of this episode, which Shaw found impossible to forget (when he was nearly ninety he went to have a look at the house in Brompton

Square where Jenny Patterson used to live), these *affaires* must have contributed to his ego-boosting. From time to time he appears to have been conscious of doubts in others as to his sexual normality. In an outburst of self-revelation to Frank Harris he said: 'If you have any doubts about my normal virility dismiss them from your mind. I was not impotent; I was not sterile; I was not homosexual; and I was extremely susceptible, though not promiscuously. . . . During the fourteen years before my marriage at forty-three there was always some lady in the case; and I tried all the experiments and learned what there was to be learned from them. The ladies were unpaid; for I had no spare money. . . . Not all my pursuers wanted sexual intercourse. Some were happily married, and appreciated our understanding that sex was barred.'

Nevertheless what is clear from Shaw's writings generally is that he attached little importance to sex. For instance, in the Preface to *Man and Superman*, written in 1903 when he was forty-seven years old, he states: 'The world's books get written, its pictures painted, its statues modelled, its symphonies composed, by people who are free from the otherwise universal dominion of the tyranny of sex. Which leads us to the conclusion – astonishing to the vulgar – that art, instead of before all things the expression of the normal sexual situation, is really the only department in which sex is a superseded and secondary power, with its consciousness so confused and its purpose so perverted, that its ideas are mere fantasy to common men.'

This is, of course, arrant nonsense: many of the world's greatest geniuses – in literature , sculpture, painting and music – were by no means indifferent to sex; on the contrary they had numerous mistresses, or, as in the case of George Sand, lovers: if assembled in parade they would form an endless procession. Abundant evidence even now is available of the sexual appetite of the geniuses in our midst. Shaw's extraordinary pronouncement, which is clearly based on his personal attitude towards sex, for he has repeatedly asserted that he is a genius, merely discloses that his own sexual virility was deficient. It can be said of Shaw that he loved women on this side of adultery.

No doubt his philandering during those years of acute disappointment at the rejection of his work helped in a measure to sustain his faith in himself and to reassure him that one day the world, too, would accept him and recognise him as a genius. That he was sexually inadequate he was able to dismiss by proclaiming that geniuses were indifferent to sex.

3
Work without Pay

PHILANDERING WITH WOMEN had made Shaw discern the difference between a theory and its practice; and he conceived the need to put the theories of Karl Marx to a practical test. That they would work he had no doubt, but he wanted to be among the first in England to bring them into operation. He realised that he would need the co-operation of others, and he found it in the house opposite the one in which he and his mother were then living in Osnaburgh Street. Here was a society that seemed ideal for the purpose: this was the Fabian Society. It had been formed only a few months earlier and its policy was clearly defined from the outset: 'For the right moment you must wait, as Fabius did most patiently, when warring against Hannibal, though many censured his delays. But when the time comes you must strike hard, as Fabius did, or your waiting will be in vain and fruitless.' Shaw joined it in 1884 and four months later his intense enthusiasm and his energy led to his being elected a member of the Executive Committee. He lost no time in roping in two other young men, both in the Civil Service and employed as clerks in the Colonial Office: one of these was Sidney Webb, the other Sydney Olivier. Annie Besant joined at about the same time.

Shaw had already equipped himself to partake in public discussions by joining a debating club known as the Zetetical Society, so called because its purpose was to enquire into the truth. His début, he tells us, was disastrous. Possessed only of 'an air of impudence', he found when he rose to his feet that he was shaking with nerves and only too conscious that he was about to make a fool of himself. Yet he went on talking because 'I could not hold my tongue'. To overcome his nervousness he spoke at every debate, no matter what was being discussed; his heart thumped noisily and his hand shook so that he was unable to read the notes he had jotted down. But he persevered. He attended the meetings of other debating societies and went to lectures to dispute the arguments of the chief speakers. 'I spoke in the streets, in the parks, at demonstrations, anywhere and everywhere possible.' At that time, he admits, he had nothing to say. But the gospel of Karl Marx was brought into full use. 'I sermonised on Socialism at least three times a fortnight average. I preached whenever and wherever I was asked.' All this provided a wider projection of his public image. Payment for speaking he refused, though he would have found the money useful. Only when he had to travel to the Provinces did he allow them to pay his third-class return railway fare. Twice he was nearly arrested by the police and was very disappointed that they had not seized him and taken him off.

To get over his nervousness was not enough, he decided. Every word, every syllable he uttered must be clearly audible, and he went into special training for this purpose. 'I practised the alphabet as a singer practises the scales.' He took lessons in elocution and in phonetic speech. His soft, gentle Irish voice thus acquired the perfect articulation of which he was justifiably proud.

Talking was not, however, the only unpaid work he did; the calls made by the Fabian Society were even more exacting: there seemed to be nothing he was not prepared to take on. He played a leading part in formulating its policy, he wrote manifestos and tracts (some of which ran to as many as twenty thousand words) and edited the *Fabian News*. Attending every meeting, he never missed an opportunity for moving resolutions and in addition went as a delegate to numerous conferences all over the country. The preparation of all the Fabian Society's publications fell to him; he handled the bulk of the correspondence, replied to the endless questions asked by members, often writing long letters in his own hand. In his very first manifesto, written in 1884, he stated that society was divided 'into hostile classes, with large appetites and no dinners at one extreme, and large dinners and no appetites at the other'. Twists and jests of this kind were used at all times to drive the argument home and make it memorable. It was an unending drudgery and he did it uncomplainingly for more than twenty years.

Mrs Margaret Cole, who, with her husband G D H Cole, was later a prominent member of the Fabian Society, wholeheartedly endorsed to me what Edward Pease, a founder-member of the Society, had said of Shaw's industry and immense output of work.

The Fabians, and Shaw with them, were drawn into a demonstration in the streets on Sunday the 13th November 1887, which came to be known as 'Bloody Sunday'. It was on behalf of the unemployed whose numbers had been rising alarmingly. One group of demonstrators, which included William Morris, Annie Besant and Shaw, assembled on Clerkenwell Green for the march on Trafalgar Square. Morris led the procession; Shaw and Mrs Besant walked together behind him, but she was warned by Shaw that if there was any trouble with the police she would have to look after herself.

In High Holborn they ran into another group of demonstrators who were being pursued and bludgeoned by the police. In the confusion one of his neighbours asked Shaw, 'What are we to do?' He replied, 'Let every man get to the square as best he can.' Annie Besant had already set off on her own. Shaw was pushed by the throng against some policemen and instantly apologised to them. John Burns, later a Member of Parliament and a Cabinet Minister, and Cunninghame-Graham, a well-known traveller and author, were arrested. Some months later when Graham was asked at a Fabian public meeting: 'Who is this Bernard Shaw?' he replied: 'He was the first man to run away from Trafalgar Square.' Shaw explained it himself in these words: 'I am a thinker, not a fighter. When the shooting begins I shall get under the bed, and not emerge until we come to real constructive business.'

Not content with these varied and exhausting Fabian activities, Shaw soon got himself elected to the St Pancras Borough Council, which was then called the Vestry, and gave long, tedious hours to dealing with the complexities of drainage and sanitation, electric lighting, housing problems and the numerous small hotels round the three great railway stations, most of which were really brothels. He had to hold inquests on tubercular cattle – the last thing, he thought, a vegetarian ought to have been asked to do – and battled relentlessly to abolish the penny that women had to pay for using a public convenience; men don't pay, why should women, he argued, and was promptly told not to be indecent. It was exhausting, but Shaw enjoyed it. 'It is good for me to be worked to the last inch whilst I last; and I love the reality of the Vestry and its dust-carts and the "H"-less orators after the silly visionary fashion-ridden theatres.' And he profited greatly from it, for the knowledge he acquired of the way people lived and struggled was put to good use in his plays; he used to say that if Shakespeare had been fortunate enough to serve on a borough council his plays would have been much more realistic and his characters more like the people one met in everyday life.

With no time to undertake anything more, Shaw nevertheless stood for election to the London County Council, but failed to get in. Nomination had got him into the Vestry, but for a faddist who denounced the normal, harmless tastes of ordinary men and women, such as eating meat, drinking a glass of beer and smoking, to expect votes was quite ludicrous, and Shaw did not try again.

A substantial strengthening of Shaw's fictitious public image was supplied by these varied and strenuous activities. His early writings on art (about which he admitted later he knew little), on music and on the theatre were so far little more than the legerdemain of a clever juggler. Now the work of public-imaging was expanded beyond all bounds and with it his showmanship became more elaborate. He began to talk of himself as a unique literary genius, whose ability not merely equalled Shakespeare's but in certain ways surpassed it; and as a progressive thinker and reformer whose brilliant brain, he indicated, had no equal.

H G Wells, who was a member of the Fabian Society, did not find Shaw easy to get on with. 'He seemed to go out of his way to seek a quarrel,' Wells told me. 'He was often quite stupidly tenacious of a line of argument and would cling to it, at times quite offensively, in order to justify himself.' I often thought Wells was like that too. There were, however, two main differences between these men; Wells, whose mother was a domestic servant and his father a gardener and also a professional cricketer, did not feel the need to create a public image: he was quite content to be what he was – a short, tubby man with blue eyes, a high piping voice, raised by his intelligence and his work to the middle-class. Ten years younger than Shaw, he was far better educated, he had worked as a pupil-teacher and studied biology under Huxley. Whereas Shaw had failed as a novelist, Wells achieved success very early and very rapidly: beginning at the age of twenty-five, within four years he had written *The Time Machine* and a great many brilliant short stories: his mental range was wider than Shaw's, it stretched from socialism to sociological romances and scientific prophesies, most of which, like the foreshadowing of the tank and of air-warfare, were fulfilled in his lifetime; and although he did not write plays, no other contemporary writer achieved so much in so many different *genres*. As hard a worker as Shaw, his output was certainly as immense: he wrote more than a hundred books in a span of activity that was fifteen years shorter than Shaw's.

The other great difference between the two was Wells's feeling that serious subjects should not be treated with levity. An instance of this is given by Wells in the course of an article on Pavlov, the Russian physiologist who was awarded the Nobel prize in 1904. Wells, who had met Pavlov and found him a 'gentle-mannered man with brown eyes', had just read his momentous book *Conditioned Reflexes*, which he described as 'a very reassuring book for those whose hopes for the future of mankind are bound up with the steadfast growth of scientific knowledge'. Regarding Pavlov as one of the greatest vivisectors, Wells was enraged by Shaw's attack, which described them all as 'these scoundrels whose habit it is to boil babies alive and see what happens'. Wells says: 'In that screaming, wildly foolish denunciation of vivisection to which I refer, Shaw, just to give his readers an idea of what vivisection meant, described one of the villains as chopping off the paws of a dog one after the other to observe its behaviour, and as being quite surprised to find that after his fourth operation there were no more paws;' and he sums up Shaw's attack in these words: 'He has made a vast jungle of shrewd commentary and dogmatic statements that collectively amount to somewhere in the region of nothing at all. . . . People call him a thinker. I doubt any consecutive thinking at all. . . . Empty he is as few of my contemporaries are empty – yes; but he echoes most sonorously in his own cathedral-like emptiness, and his outward effect is striking and entertaining, not simply to himself, but to us all.' A scathing onslaught on Shaw's misconceptions, mixed, as it often was, with what Wells calls his 'vivid misconceptions about life'.

Bertrand Russell told me: 'Shaw was certainly very clever, but he was not a wise man. In many ways he was rather silly and childish.'

4
Diversions

Dᴜʀɪɴɢ ᴛʜᴇsᴇ ʏᴇᴀʀs of crowded activity Shaw met a large number of people, but he was left with little time to form friendships. Nevertheless there was a drawing together of a few of them in a more intimate association in a social setting provided by one of the more affluent of their members. William Morris, a poet remembered today for his *Earthly Paradise* and his socialistic work *News from Nowhere*, was twenty-two years Shaw's senior. A handsome man with a taste for blue shirts, he revolutionised the décor of the Victorian home by designing a distinctive type of furniture and brilliantly coloured wallpaper patterned with tropical flowers and exotic birds. In addition to his house in Hammersmith in London, he had a country mansion, Kelmscott Manor, in Gloucestershire, where, interlarding work with diversion, the Fabians used to meet to listen to lectures in the converted coach-house. Most of these lectures were given by Shaw; and it was there that he met Morris's very beautiful young daughter May, whose portrait was painted by Burne-Jones. Shaw has recorded the meeting. 'I looked at her, rejoicing in the lovely dress and lovely self; and she looked at me very carefully and quite deliberately made a gesture of assent with her eyes. I was immediately conscious that a Mystic Betrothal was registered in heaven, to be fulfilled when all material obstacles should melt away, and my own position rescued from the squalors of my poverty and unsuccess; for subconsciously I had no doubt of my rank as a man of genius.... I did not think it necessary to say anything....

It did not occur to me even that fidelity to the Mystical Betrothal need interfere with the ordinary course of my relations with other women. I made no sign at all: I had no doubt that the thing was written in the skies for both of us.' The year was 1885 when his love affair with Jenny Patterson cost him his virginity.

He said nothing to May during their subsequent meetings although it was quite apparent that they were in love with each other. He need not have been conscious of his poverty; he had begun to earn money by writing for the newspapers, and anyway May had enough money to keep them both in ample comfort.

Tired of waiting for him to speak, May eventually accepted a proposal of marriage from Henry Sparling, an employee of her father who was even poorer than Shaw – 'to my utter stupefaction', Shaw writes, and adds that it was 'entirely my own fault'.

May, and apparently her husband too, invited Shaw to stay with them because he had been working too hard and needed rest badly. 'Everything went well for a time in that *ménage à trois*. She was glad to have me in the house; and he was glad to have me because I kept her in good humour. . . . But the violated Betrothal was avenging itself. It made me from the outset the centre of the household; and when I had quite recovered and there was no longer any excuse for staying, unless I proposed to do so permanently and parasitically, her legal marriage dissolved as all illusions do.' The husband vanished and so did Shaw – 'I knew that a scandal would damage us both.' Shaw wrote this version of their romance for May when they were both old and she used it in the last volume of her father's collected works, saying that it was better to have a frank first-hand account of their romance than to have the whole thing distorted later by someone else.

Another member of the Fabian Society who brought some of the members together in a social setting was Beatrice Potter, who married Shaw's friend Sidney Webb in 1892 and was herself a Fabian. Her father was an exceedingly rich railway magnate: he was Chairman of the Great Western Railway in England and President of the Grand Trunk Railway in Canada, and had widespread interests in numerous other industrial enterprises. Beatrice, one of nine daughters, acted as hostess for her father and entertained such prominent Victorian thinkers as Huxley, Herbert Spencer, Tyndall, Hooker and the novelist George Eliot. Despite her affluent upbringing Beatrice was drawn to socialism when she became aware of the poverty and suffering of the enormous number of families who were living in slums. Her way of entertaining was by renting a house in the country (usually a rectory) for some weeks in the spring or summer, and often again in the autumn, and inviting a group of Fabians there. While this had about it something of the atmosphere of a country-house party, a substantial amount of time was spent by the hostess and the guests in discussions. Schedules of work were drawn up and hours were devoted to discussing plans for the betterment of the condition of the poor, and reshaping the political framework for the advantage of the people. Diversion was not completely ignored. Intervals were provided for long country walks and for bicycling which had just become the great rage. They all took this up – little tubby Sidney Webb with his small goatee beard, slender, stern, domineering Beatrice, very tall, powerfully built Graham Wallas, and Sydney Olivier, a civil-servant friend of Sidney Webb. Shaw got a bicycle, too, and spent a great deal of time learning to ride it. Bertrand Russell, who was often one of the guests, has told me of an occasion in Monmouthshire when he and Shaw set out together on a bicycle ride. Shaw, he discovered, had not really mastered the cycle. 'He wobbled uncertainly and dangerously and it seemed to me a folly to embark on this ride with him. I decided to keep well ahead of him to avoid a collision, but as Shaw knew the countryside and I didn't, I found I had to dismount at every fork and at all the crossroads, and wait for him to tell me which one to take.

'At one fork, while I waited, Shaw came swooping down the hill towards me. I could see he was unable to stop and my thoughts went back to our talk that morning of his dream of becoming a great playwright. As he swept calamitously down I realised that his dream was unlikely to be fulfilled. He wobbled, his machine zigzagged, and ended up by crashing into my bicycle. The impact lifted him right out of his seat and shot him twenty feet ahead, where he lay spread-eagled on the roadway.

' "That's the end of Shaw," I thought. I rushed up to see what I could do, but felt that it was already too late. On coming nearer I saw that he was still alive, for he had begun to stir and was attempting to rise. He limped towards his bicycle, which, miraculously, was almost undamaged, he mounted it and, without so much as a glance at me, rode off, quite determined apparently to keep ahead of me this time. My bicycle was a complete wreck. The wheels were twisted, the frame was bent. It was impossible for me to ride it. There was nothing I could do except finish the journey by train.'

The nearest railway station was a mile or so away. Bertrand Russell, after a wait there, got into a slow local train which crawled its way through the countryside. 'It was an unpleasant journey. I had brought nothing to read. But what was even more painful was to see the tall, slender, bearded figure of Shaw pedalling furiously beside the train, overtaking it at intervals, and whenever he came to my window, bellowing, *yah*-ing and jeering at me – a not very becoming performance by a man sixteen years your senior.'

Among the other Fabians who attended these country-house gatherings was Henry Salt, who had been a master at Eton, but preferred to live in a labourer's cottage in Tilford, in the Surrey hills. Shaw went to stay there from time to time and they set out on long country walks together. On one awful occasion Shaw had to walk in the drenching rain from Farnham station to the cottage, his sleeves wet and sticking to his wrists: 'I looked down at my clinging knees, and instantly discharged a pint of rain-water and black dye over them from my hat brim.' He was not a good house-guest. Those with whom he stayed found him a busybody who interfered ceaselessly with their way of life. 'Before you know where you are,' one of them complained, 'he has chosen a school for your son, made your will for you, regulated your diet, and assumed all the privileges of your family solicitor, your housekeeper, your clergyman, your doctor, your dressmaker, your hairdresser, and your estate agent. When he has finished with everyone else he incites the children to rebellion.'

Another friendship Shaw formed at that time was with Ellen Terry, but it was a friendship confined to paper. His first letter to her was written in 1892; it was a reply ('exceedingly stiff and prim,' she called it) to a letter about a young singer she had sent to Yates, Shaw's editor on *The World*. The correspondence went on for years; they did not meet until it had virtually ended.

Shaw had, of course, seen her on the stage soon after his arrival in London, when he was twenty and Ellen Terry eight years his senior. He found her enchanting and never missed a play in which she appeared; in his dramatic criticisms his praise of her acting was ecstatic. Quite early he formed the resolve to persuade her to appear in one of *his* plays. She was at that time the most beautiful and outstanding actress on the English stage.

His letters, seemingly from a man deeply in love, were in fact no more than a pleasant platonic exercise, full of wit and autobiographical revelations. Ellen Terry's letters, too, quite often achieved a very high standard. But the possibility of using her was uppermost in Shaw's mind. He sent her *The Man of Destiny*, hoping that Henry Irving, with whom she had been performing at the Lyceum Theatre for nearly twenty years, would play

Napoleon and Ellen the Strange Lady—he had written the rôle specially for her. Irving, however, did not like the play; indeed he did not like Shaw and generally referred to him as 'Your Mr Pshaw!' It was not until 1906, when she was nearly sixty, that Ellen Terry appeared for the first and only time in a Shaw play – *Captain Brassbound's Conversion*, which was written in 1900 for her. But she disliked the part of Lady Cecily ('she gets her way in everything – just like you,' Shaw told her) and when the play was produced later that year the rôle was taken by another actress, Janet Achurch, with whom Shaw had been philandering some years earlier. Six years later Ellen, by now a grandmother, read the play again and was glad to appear in it, accepting the ridiculously small salary of £5 a week as against the £200 a week she had got in her heyday. Thanks to her fine performance the play was a success and she later took it on tour.

Shaw says of this friendship: 'Ellen Terry and I exchanged about two hundred and fifty letters in the nineties. An old-fashioned governess would say that many of them were wild love-letters; and yet, though we were all the time within a shilling hansom-ride of one another's doors, we never saw one another in private; and the only time I ever touched her was on the first night of *Brassbound*, when I formally kissed her hand.' Ellen had caught a glimpse of him in 1896 by looking through the peephole of the Lyceum Theatre curtain: 'I've seen you at last,' she wrote. 'You are a boy, and a duck.' He was forty at the time and she was nearly fifty. It was their deliberate decision not to meet for fear that the reality might spoil the illusion. She dreaded it, and Shaw agreed. He wrote to her: 'I, too, fear to break the spell; remorses, presentiments, all sorts of tendernesses wring my heart at the thought of materialising this beautiful friendship of ours by a meeting.' The rehearsals of *Captain Brassbound* brought them together. 'After the play was disposed of,' Shaw states, 'our meetings were few. . . . She was

43

always a little shy in speaking to me; for talking hampered by material circumstances is awkward and unsatisfactory after the perfect freedom of writing between people who can write.'

Ellen Terry died in 1928 and the letters were published, with a long preface by Shaw, in the following year. Neither Shaw's wife, Charlotte, nor Ellen Terry's son, Gordon Craig, was pleased that the correspondence was made public.

Occasionally his work as a Socialist or a dramatic critic took Shaw abroad. He disliked travelling. In September, when he went to Venice with the Art-Workers Guild, he complained almost ceaselessly in his letters to William Morris and others. His growing irritation was caused 'by these twenty-seven men, about twenty of whom seem to me to be capable of admiring everything except beauty'. One of them, Sydney Cockerell, who was described by Shaw as having his face and neck used as 'a mosquito pasture – all red spots,' later became a close friend of his, and the Curator of the Fitzwilliam Museum in Cambridge.

But these were not Shaw's only diversions, nor did his political and Borough activities debar him from other strenuous mental pursuits. He had already begun to write plays, and, as with his novels, he went on writing them, although no commercial theatre manager was prepared to put them on. (These will be dealt with in another chapter.) Chief of his other diversions was music. Shaw had grown up in a home that was filled with music. His mother sang, his elder sister Lucy sang. Lee organised concerts and produced operas. So a knowledge and love of music became inevitably a part of his life. He taught himself to play the piano and played it tolerably well. He was considered good enough by that great pianist Harriet Cohen to play a piano duet with her. The self-tuition began after the home in Dublin was broken up and his mother and sisters had left for London. 'Music had been my daily food,' and suddenly there was no more of it. But fortunately the piano was still there. 'I had never touched it,' he states, 'except to pick out a tune with one finger. In desperation I bought a technical handbook of music, containing a diagram of the keyboard. I then got out my mother's vocal score of *Don Giovanni*, and tried to play the overture. It took me some minutes to arrange my fingers on the notes of the first chord. What I suffered, what everybody in the house suffered' – meaning no doubt his father when he was at home, drunk, and possibly a woman who helped with the cleaning and cooking – 'whilst I struggled on, labouring through arrangements of Beethoven's symphonies, and vocal scores of all the operas and oratorios I knew, will never be told. In the end I learned enough to thumb my way through anything. I never mastered the keyboard; but I did a good deal of rum-tum accompanying in my first days in London, and even once, in a desperate emergency, supplied the place of the absent half of the orchestra at a performance of *Il Trovatore* at a People's Entertainment evening at the Victoria Theatre in the Waterloo Road (the Old Vic) and came off without disaster, and in fact mostly imposed my own *tempi* on the amiable and unassertive Italian conductor.'

He kept up his piano-playing until the end of his life. During his last years, his housekeeper, Mrs Alice Laden, told me, he used to come down from his bedroom after everyone had gone to bed and would sit at the cottage piano at the foot of the stairs and play happily for two hours or more, Mozart chiefly and sometimes Beethoven. He had a pleasant singing voice – during his office-boy period in the estate office in Dublin he used to assemble the 'gentlemen apprentices', as he liked to call them, and when the boss was out taught them to sing scraps from the operas. Mrs Laden remembers that quite often, after a long spell of opera on the piano, he would suddenly switch to London music-hall ditties and Irish ballads and raise his lusty voice in song, to the despair of Mrs Laden and the two housemaids.

Music was for him a glorious immersion in the beauty of sound. Even as a teenage clerk after a long day at the office, while other boys dashed off to play cricket or football, he would salvage a shilling or two out of his sparse income to spend an evening listening to an opera. And it was his music and the love of sound that led to his ceaseless interest in achieving the most euphonious use of the spoken word, which made his voice one of the most beautiful to listen to.

5
Marriage

AMONG THE FABIANS at Beatrice Webb's country-house parties in the mid-nineties was an Irishwoman named Charlotte Payne-Townshend, aged about forty, with an elegant and affluent family background which Shaw found most impressive. It was a background that he would have classified as being less exalted than his own, for her family lacked a baronet; but of her wealth there could be no doubt. In Shaw's mind it far surpassed the most exaggerated notions of the fortune possessed by the ennobled senior line of the Shaw family, for Sir Robert Shaw left less than £5,000 when he died and his brother who succeeded him left less than £3,000; whereas Miss Payne-Townshend at the end of her comfortable life, in which she denied herself and her husband nothing, left more than £150,000.

From the moment of their meeting, Shaw referred repeatedly to her in his letters. He described her to Ellen Terry as a green-eyed Irish millionairess – 'a great catch for somebody.... I am going to refresh my heart by falling in love with her. I love falling in love – but, mind, only with her, not with the millions; somebody else must marry her if she can stand him after me.' She was not pretty. In one of his letters Shaw said: 'She is, normally, a ladylike person at whom nobody would ever look twice, so perfectly does she fit into her place . . . perfectly placid and proper and pleasant.' Under that placidity an emotional turmoil raged within her. She had been unhappy in her childhood. Her domineering mother bullied her father in order to attain her social ambitions.

First 'Payne' was added to the family surname of 'Townsend', then an 'H' was inserted into the latter. In the end she forced him to give up the old family estate at Derry, which he loved, and they moved to England. Charlotte's sympathies were with her father and from time to time she quarrelled with her mother over her treatment of him. It may be that this atmosphere of marital unhappiness and unrest had set her thoughts against marriage, for after a childhood of elaborate and selective entertaining, during which her younger sister 'Sissy' (christened Mary Stewart) found a husband, Charlotte, to her mother's intense annoyance and distress, remained unmarried, though suitors had not been lacking. Her father died when she was nineteen; he arranged that his widow should enjoy only the income until her death, after which his great wealth, consisting of estates, farms, shares in banks, railways, gas and other companies, should be divided equally between his two daughters.

By the time Charlotte met Shaw she had already come into her inheritance and thus was a woman of complete independence. She had not yet shed her love for riding and hunting, and the restlessness inherited from her mother took her on many visits to the Continent. In Rome, while staying with friends, she met the attractive Swedish doctor Axel Munthe, a man of striking personality who already, at the age of thirty-four, had a large, fashionable clientele; but what drew Charlotte to him was his readiness to sacrifice the fat fees of rich women to go into an epidemic-ridden slum to minister to the poor; for Charlotte herself possessed a strong quixotic strain. She was seeking a way of life that would help her to disentangle the twisted strands of her personality. Munthe, she felt, could help her to attain this. Embedded in this quest was a deep religious undertone, in no way identifiable with any recognisable conventional religion. She wanted a spiritual satisfaction, a fulfilment that no known religion was able to provide.

Munthe had studied hypnotism with Jean-Martin

Charcot and found this useful for the treatment of hysteria; but his personality was in itself powerfully compulsive and he had no need to resort to hypnosis in his relations with Charlotte or any other of the women who swarmed round him. He had been married, but his young wife had divorced him before his meeting with Charlotte. In his home on the Piazza di Spagna, where the poet Keats had once lived, Charlotte often visited him. He told her that there was nothing really the matter with her, but she must learn to control her nerves. He suggested a change of air. He said that he was going to Venice to attend the Crown Princess of Sweden and that it would be pleasant if Charlotte went there too. They saw each other many times in Venice. He was intelligent, vital and talked most interestingly. After a fortnight Charlotte returned to Rome and they saw each other again. They lunched and dined quite often and there is no doubt, though she may have been unable to analyse her emotions in that way, that she was falling in love with him. He was sympathetic and understanding and she told him a great deal of her early life and her search for contentment. He admired her intelligence, her incessant quest for knowledge and the forceful way in which she expressed herself. He became aware too of her strong sense of injustice and her eagerness to better the conditions of the poor, for which purpose she was always ready to use her money. He took her to visit the Little Sisters of the Poor and she subscribed readily to help their work. But nothing came of this growing attachment. Munthe left Rome. Their meetings came to an end. She wrote, but he rarely replied and in time their letters ceased.

Shortly after her return to London she met Beatrice Webb. Finding that Charlotte's interests were similar to her own ('She is a socialist and radical,' Mrs Webb noted in her diary), it was not difficult for her to extract a subscription of £1,000 for the London School of Economics, which the Webbs had just established. To identify herself more closely with the work Charlotte moved into a large flat above the School at 10 Adelphi Terrace. Shortly afterwards she joined the Fabian Society and her meeting with Shaw followed; they talked, they argued, Shaw often mocked at her ideas and this greatly irritated her.

Beatrice noticed that mingled with Charlotte's charm were 'certain volcanic tendencies'; but nevertheless Shaw and she went cycling together, just the two of them, Charlotte large, heavy-shouldered, auburn-haired, Shaw very thin and tall, pale-faced, red-bearded, mischief dancing in his brilliantly blue eyes.

Despite his letters to Ellen Terry and his harping on her being 'an Irish millionairess', it can hardly be said that Shaw embarked at once on any form of courtship. His diary notes, on the 20th March 1897: 'Miss Payne-Townshend "At Home" to London School of Economics. Did not go.' A few days later Charlotte went to Rome again, where she constantly heard talk of Munthe's activities. He was building a house for himself in Anacapri, which he later called San Michele, and wrote a book about his life there. Charlotte listened, and often thought of their meetings and their talks together. In August both she and Shaw were among the Webbs' guests at Saxmundham. Again they bicycled together, sometimes alone, sometimes with others. In the evenings Shaw read his latest play to the assembled guests and they discussed it or spent the time elaborating fresh political schemes.

Beatrice Webb, who had known Shaw to be in love with so many women, at no time thought that he was in love with Charlotte. He had recently been going about with the actress Janet Achurch; she was married to an actor named Charrington, but that did not deter Shaw. He used to sit up at night writing his long infatuated letters to her, full of his admiration, interspersed with his inevitable lecturing. One evening he found her 'the worse for drink; and I had to talk religion to calm her'. On another occasion Janet and her husband were angrily engaged in throwing crockery at each other. Charrington, who had apparently made no attempt to discourage the close friendship between Shaw and Janet, was not surprised now to see him join in the quarrel. Gazing at the fragments of crockery on the carpet, Shaw said: 'Leave some for tomorrow.' But Charrington replied: 'There is not going to be a tomorrow. You can have Janet.'

Overlapping with Janet, Shaw had begun to visit an artist called Bertha Newcombe. A great deal of his time was spent in her studio in Chelsea, and he was seen 'everywhere' with her. Beatrice Webb took this new involvement a great deal better than any of his earlier ones. She felt that it would be a good thing if Shaw would marry Bertha, who was happily a Fabian, and settle down at last. Charlotte she earmarked as a suitable wife for Graham Wallas, another prominent Fabian at her house-parties. To further both projects she invited all four, Wallas and Charlotte, Shaw and Bertha, to stay at the Rectory at Saxmundham that summer. When Bertha told Shaw of her invitation, he firmly advised her not to go and said that he was thinking of staying away himself. Thus discouraged, Bertha wrote to Beatrice that she was unable to come. But Shaw went, pleased with his ruse to prevent Charlotte and Bertha meeting.

By now he had begun to write letters to Charlotte. They were long and affectionate, as all his letters were to the women he selected for his philandering. 'Keep me deep in your heart. Write me two lines whenever you love me' – yet one doubts if he had any thought of marrying her. Charlotte seemed to enjoy his company. Beatrice Webb recorded in her diary that Charlotte 'bitterly resents her enforced celibacy, but thinks she could not tolerate the matter-of-fact side of marriage'. Still, though her response to Shaw's outpourings were often cool, she was interested enough in him to let him make her his unpaid secretary. He sent her his plays to type and indeed had other women doing the same thing. Shaw's income had by now begun to improve but he was

51

in no position to employ a full-time secretary. He still lived with his mother in an upstairs room cluttered with books and papers, covered with dust because no one was allowed to touch them.

It was at this stage that Bertha Newcombe, deeply worried about the change in Shaw's manner towards her, appealed to Beatrice Webb to come and see her. Beatrice went to the Chelsea studio and has recorded their talk in her diary. 'She is *petite* and dark – about forty years old but looks more like a wizened girl than a fully developed woman. Her jet-black hair heavily fringed, half smart, half artistic clothes, pinched aquiline features and thin lips. . . . "I want to talk to you, Mrs Webb," she said, when I had seated myself. And then followed, told with the dignity of devoted feeling, the story of her relationship to Bernard Shaw, her five years' devoted love, his cold philandering, her hopes aroused by my repeated advice to him (which he, it appears, had repeated to her much exaggerated) to marry her – and then her feeling of dismay and resentment against me when she discovered that I was encouraging him to marry Miss Townshend! Finally he had written a month ago to break it off entirely. . . . And I had to explain to her with perfect frankness that so long as there seemed a chance for her I had been willing to act as chaperone . . . and that as far as I was concerned I should have welcomed her as his wife. But directly I saw that he meant nothing I backed out of the affair. She took it all quietly – her little face seemed to shrink up. . . . "You are well out of it, Miss Newcombe," I said gently. "If you had married Shaw he would not have remained faithful to you. . . . In his relations with women he is vulgar – if not worse – it is a vulgarity which includes cruelty and springs from vanity." As I uttered these words my eyes caught her portrait of Shaw – full-length, with red-gold hair and laughing blue eyes and his mouth slightly open as if scoffing at us both – a powerful picture in which the love of the woman had given genius to the artist. Her little face turned to follow my eyes and she felt also the expression of the man – the mockery at her deep-rooted affection.' Many years later Bertha Newcombe, writing of her association with Shaw, described him as 'a passionless man. He had passed through experiences, and he seemed to have no wish for, and even to fear, passion, though he admitted its power and pleasure. . . . Frequent talking, talking of the pros and cons of marriage, even to my prospects of money or the want of it, his dislike of the sexual relation and so on, would create an atmosphere of love-making without any need for caresses or endearments.'

To Ellen Terry, Shaw was writing at this time that Charlotte 'insists on coming to my lectures in all sorts of holes and corners – dock-gates next Sunday morning. I have noticed that the experience makes her very unhappy. . . . It appears that my demagogic denunciation of the idle rich – my demands for taxation of unearned income – lacerated her conscience, for she has great possessions. What am I to do? She won't stay away; and I can't talk Primrose League.' That was not true. Shaw had in fact to coax Charlotte to come to these meetings; he did so again and again: and in any case, as a Socialist and Fabian, she was not in the least likely to have her conscience lacerated by what he said, or to want to listen to talk about the Conservative Primrose League – and no one knew that better than Shaw.

By the autumn Beatrice had noticed that Charlotte 'is deeply attached to him. But I see no sign on his side of the growth of any geniune or steadfast affection. He finds it pleasant to be with her in her luxuriant surroundings. . . . He has been flattered by her devotion and absorption in him. . . . There are ominous signs that he is tired of watching the effect of little words of gallantry and personal interest with which he plied her in the first months of the friendship.'

But Shaw's letters to Charlotte continued – as well as his letters to Ellen Terry. He wrote to Ellen in the autumn of 1897 after a house-party: 'Down at Dorking there was a sort of earthquake because she' – meaning Charlotte – 'had been cherishing a charming project of at last making me a very cherishing and romantic proposal – saving it up as a sort of climax to the proofs she was giving me every day of her regard for me. When I received that golden moment with shuddering horror and wildly asked for the fare to Australia she was inexpressibly taken aback, and her pride, which is considerable, was much startled.' The whole of this is untrue: its very inconsistency reveals that. Charlotte's 'considerable pride' would surely have prevented her from taking the undignified step of risking a rebuff, seeing that Shaw, as Beatrice Webb records, 'always advertised his views on marriage and philandering from the house-tops'.

Though he told Ellen he wanted to run away from Charlotte, he was in fact writing to her at the time in much more affectionate terms. 'Ever Dearest', his letter dated the 14th November 1897 began, and he went on without further ado to describe an accident in which he was involved. 'I had a toss on the big hill on the way home; but I was not hurt except for a black-eye and a cut face; so do not be alarmed by the blood-curdling account I am sending to Mrs Phillimore' – with whom Charlotte was then staying in Hertfordshire. 'A woman got into my way when I was going fast down the hill. I managed to twist the bike round her safely, but . . . literally wiped the floor with my left cheek. I am a ludicrous spectacle – like a badly defeated prize-fighter. I rode on gaily to Edgware, called a doctor there, got stitched up, and rode home.' He was always describing his state of health in his letters, possibly to win sympathy, and he ended this one to Charlotte with the words: 'I am glad I got just enough hurt to make you tender to me.' When later she was away in Rome he wrote to tell her that he had an acute toothache and had been to the dentist. 'Tooth sacrificed in vain. Not toothache–neuralgia,' and he went on moaning about not having her services as his secretary.

54

Things came to a head in an odd way. On the 18th April 1898 he wrote to Charlotte, who was still in Rome, to say that his left foot was swollen. 'Don't understand it. Seems to be positively putrefying.' The next day he wrote again: 'I find my left foot unaccountably sore and have to take off my shoe. Not easy to get it on again. Ride home. On taking off the shoe again, my foot expands to the size of a leg of mutton. Don't understand it, as there is nothing to account for it but the fact that a week or so ago I laced my shoe too tight and pinched my instep a little.' During the succeeding days the foot got steadily worse and he was unable to walk without suffering acute pain. His work made it essential for him to get about. On the 21st he wrote: 'Locomotion now very excruciating. Can it be gout? Looks awful. Have to lunch at home and not stir until the theatre in the evening. Spite of cabs the theatre makes it decidedly worse. Foot now as large as the Albert Hall. . . . Am a fearful wreck.'

He wrote every day. The condition of his foot was the one note he harped on. Charlotte left Rome at the end of April and travelled from Naples by sea, arriving in London late at night on the 1st May. Shaw had gone to meet her train at Charing Cross and, not finding her on it, hobbled along to her flat in Adelphi Terrace. He was in a fury. The maid asked him if he would care to wait as she was expected just after midnight. 'Clearly I cannot. I limp back to my bus, and here I am,' he wrote to her on getting home.

Charlotte went to see him the next afternoon and climbed up to the little room on the second floor in his mother's house at 29 Fitzroy Square. She was appalled. It was a very small room. She had been told by Shaw that his mother was not interested in housekeeping, but she had thought that the servant might at least have kept the room clean. There was dirt and disorder everywhere. The plates on which he had had his meals were still lying about unwashed. His mother never bothered to come into his room, nor had she made any effort to deal with his swollen foot. Charlotte saw that Shaw was looking ill and haggard. The doctor had discovered an abscess on his instep and had lanced it. With an assertive emphasis Charlotte announced that she was going to look after him herself. She would take a house in the country, she said, and would take him there with her. Up to the end of his life Shaw always insisted that he could not have accepted the offer to live alone under the same roof as Charlotte without causing a scandal, and that was really why he married her.

Both Charlotte and Shaw had strong views about marrying. She had been greatly upset as a child by the unhappiness of her father's life with her mother; yet had Munthe proposed there was the possibility that she might have accepted him. It was also thought likely that the marital bliss existing between Sidney and Beatrice Webb may have encouraged the hope that perhaps marriage with Shaw would not be a failure. And Shaw, being a philanderer, never wanted to be tied to any one woman, though Charlotte's gentle birth, and above all her wealth, may have adjusted his thoughts a little.

They were married on the 1st June 1898 at the West Strand Registrar's office in Henrietta Street. Shaw was not quite forty-two, Charlotte six months younger. The bridegroom arrived on crutches, wearing an old shabby jacket. Charlotte's cousin, Edith Somerville, the Irish writer who together with Martin Ross wrote *The Experiences of an Irish RM*, was most surprised to hear of it and described the marriage as a misalliance. 'He is an advanced socialist,' she wrote to a friend, 'all the same he has kept his weather eye open. He can't be a gentleman and he is too clever to be really in love with Lollie.'

For years he kept telling his friends that it was Charlotte who married him. Towards the close of his life, when he was in his nineties, he rang the bell in the dining-room with his foot (the button was under the carpet by his chair) and asked the maid to send in Mrs

Alice Laden, who had nursed Charlotte when she died and was acting as his housekeeper at Ayot St Lawrence.

'I wondered what on earth the maid had forgotten to take in for his dinner,' she told me. 'I went into the room and found that it had nothing to do with the meal. He had already finished eating and was standing by the fireplace when I came in.

'He asked me to sit down: he sometimes did that when he wanted to talk. It was usually some memory out of the past, for though in his plays, his other writings and his talk he was always trying to plan the future for everybody, whether they liked it or not, he often dwelt on the past too, certainly during the years I was with him.

'Quite abruptly, without any preamble or introductory remarks at all, he said: "I never proposed to my wife, you know. It was she who proposed to me and carried me off to marry her." He chuckled then. "I arrived on crutches and I had leather patches on the elbows of my jacket. One look at me and the registrar decided that I couldn't possibly be the bridegroom. So he married Charlotte to Henry Salt, one of the two witnesses who had come to sign the register. I was enjoying this. But in the end I walked off with the prize." '

Shaw's memory must have been heavily troubled by the fact that Charlotte had made all the arrangements. She went to Fitzroy Square and packed his papers and books, she rented a house at Pitfold, between Haslemere and Hindhead, and there they lived for four months while Shaw had a convalescing honeymoon. When they returned to London, he moved into her home at 10 Adelphi Terrace. Charlotte was well aware that Shaw was not able to keep her on the money he was earning, certainly not in the style to which she had been accustomed. So the money arrangements were discussed quite frankly. She felt that Shaw's mother would need some financial help, for although for years he had given her hardly anything, of late he had been making some contribution. Charlotte arranged to settle an annuity of

£400 on her for life. With regard to their own expenses, it was decided that each would pay a proportion of the cost of running the home. Shaw had simple tastes and was able to manage on very little. Charlotte had always lived extravagantly. She dressed well, a great deal of her money was spent on her clothes. She liked entertaining and travelling, always stayed in the best hotels when she went abroad or rented a comfortable country house for a holiday in England. Shaw wanted none of this: he preferred to stay where he was and to get on with his work.

Of his marriage Shaw wrote in 1930 a chapter entitled 'To Frank Harris on Sex in Biography', which appears in Shaw's *Sixteen Self Sketches*: 'Not until I was past forty did I earn enough to marry without seeming to marry for money, nor did my wife at the same age without suspicion of being driven by sex-starvation. As man and wife we found a new relation in which sex had no part. It ended the old gallantries, flirtations and philanderings for both of us. Even of these it was the ones that were never consummated that left the longest and kindliest memories. Do not forget that all marriages are different, and that marriages between young people, followed by parentage, must not be lumped in with childless partnerships between middle-aged people who have passed the age at which the bride can safely bear a first child.' Some of this, written thirteen years before Charlotte's death, though not published until after it, is singularly unfair to her. The reference to her not being driven to marriage by sex-starvation implies, and this is supported by a later phrase, that she too had given up 'her gallantries and philanderings', that she had, like him, indulged in pre-marital sex relationships. It is unlikely that there is any truth in this. We know that Charlotte had told him about Axel Munthe, but it is doubtful that it went any further than an infatuation on her side. As for Shaw abandoning his philanderings, this too is utterly untrue. The affair with Mrs Patrick Campbell, which many believe did have a sexual outlet, occurred after his marriage; it is dealt with in a later chapter.

That there was a possessive love on Charlotte's side is undoubted. She was a devoted wife. She ministered materially, even lavishly, to all his wants. She acted as his secretary in the early years, undertook the research for all his historical plays and often found some of the subjects for him, in particular *St Joan*. Mrs Laden told me that she used sometimes to sit in a chair outside his door while he worked in his London flat so as to prevent any noise disturbing him – the noise of the Hoover, for instance, or whispered talk by the domestic staff. Shaw's attitude to Charlotte was always one of gratefulness for all she did for him. But he did not really understand her, nor make any effort to do so. Both were deeply religious in their different ways and if Shaw had attempted to reconcile the two standpoints there would have been a substantial area they could have explored together. He kept on proclaiming that he was an atheist, though later he appears to have abandoned this stance after substituting the 'Life Force' for God. Some of her friends believed that Charlotte was a Christian Scientist, but she was not. She had made a very close and searching study of Ouspensky's *Esoterism and Modern Thought* as well as his *Tertium Organum*, as the large quantity of notes she left show. Towards the close of her life she wrote to a friend in California: 'To me PS and T' – these initials have not been identified – 'has been a revelation. A spark that lighted up the whole pile of little personal discoveries and made them glow with new lights. It just put the final pinnacle on the edifice built up by me from Ouspensky and all the others.... I have been more or less studying all this since before I gave you the little Gita at Kilteragh, and I soon found out all you say about its demanding *everything*. At first one thinks of a quarter of an hour a day, and soon one finds it means one's life and being and loyalty. There was a time when, if I had been free, I would have given up everything else for it.'

She revealed her innermost thoughts in her letters to T E Lawrence, and when Shaw read them after her death he was utterly shocked. 'She poured out her soul to Lawrence,' he wrote. 'There were parts of her character that even I did not know. . . . Of all the women I have known (and I have known many) I knew Charlotte least of all.'

Often they sat quietly side by side at home, hardly exchanging a word; whenever she tried to express an opinion on some pet subject of his, he would dismiss it, saying, 'You don't know what you're talking about.' But at other times their relationship was most pleasant. Barry Jackson, the theatrical impresario who put on the Shaw Festivals at Malvern during the thirties, dropped in one evening at Whitehall Court and found them seated on a sofa, looking at a picture-book together; and often, before going to bed, he would make up amusing parodies of well-known music-hall ditties to divert her. These were moments of companionship of which they had many during the stresses and anxieties of the many travels on which Charlotte dragged him. But Mrs Laden recalls that they never spoke at meal-times when they were alone. Shaw liked silence and the rule was strictly observed.

'I was called in to nurse her six months before she died,' Mrs Laden told me. 'I was with her at Ayot St Lawrence for a time and then she came up to Whitehall Court. She never liked Ayot, and Mr Shaw never liked the way she did the drawing-room there. He always used the dining-room for entertaining his friends and worked in the study at the foot of the stairs or in the hut at the end of the garden. Hers was a long and sad illness. She was quite a big woman normally, but she had shrunk to half her size. The doctors diagnosed her illness as "osteitis deformans", due, they said, to an accident she had had in her teens, apparently while out riding.

'Very early in the morning of the day she died Mrs Shaw, who had some of Mr Shaw's typed sheets in her room, got out of her large Hepplewhite four-poster bed and gathered the papers in her arms, but, being unsteady on her legs, she stumbled and fell. Her head hit a sewing-table by the bed and was badly gashed. Had she fallen on the other side her head would have struck the marble fireplace and she would have died. Hearing her fall, I ran into the room to pick her up. On the floor beside her was the small bedside clock and a bottle of sleeping-pills. She was stone cold. I tried to pick her up, but she was so heavy that I was unable to lift her and ran to get help. Two of the attendants at Whitehall Court came running to the flat and we picked her up and put her back into bed. I surrounded her with hot-water bottles, but after a time I noticed that her face was beginning to swell.

'I went to Mr Shaw's room and told him what had happened. He said: "She has often fallen on the floor."

' "But, Mr Shaw," I said, "this is different. It is serious." He looked at me vaguely. I wondered if he had really taken it in. His manner was generally very casual as he did not like to show emotion.' One could wonder if he was capable of personal emotion, as distinct from written emotion, which included, of course, his exercises in philandering.

'By the evening Mrs Shaw said she felt better and insisted on coming out to join her husband at dinner. The two sat together at the table. She spoke to him twice, but his thoughts seemed to be elsewhere, for he didn't answer. The first time she just looked at him, but when she addressed him again and once again he ignored it, she got up from the table and I assisted her to her room. It was obvious that she was annoyed. He asked, "What is the matter, Charlotte?" but she did not answer.

'A few minutes later he came to her bedroom and entered without knocking. I was busy undressing her to get her ready for bed. Mr Shaw repeated: "What's the matter, Charlotte?" but she ignored him. He stayed for a few minutes and then left. When I came out of the room he stopped me and asked if I knew what had upset her. I explained that she had spoken to him twice but had received no reply. "I never heard her," he said. "I'll go in and tell her so." He went to the room and was there for a short while. It was their last talk together, for a little later that night she died. By ten o'clock Mrs Shaw was in a coma. She seemed nevertheless to be fighting for her life.'

Charlotte died ten minutes after midnight – it was by then Sunday, the 12th September 1943. She was eighty-six. Mrs Laden went to inform Shaw, who was in bed. He just looked at her, without getting up to go to Charlotte's room.

Early the next morning Mrs Laden found him on his knees by the four-poster bed, with his hands clasped in prayer. He kept returning to the room and on one occasion Mrs Laden saw him seated on the bed gazing at Charlotte. Aware that someone had come in, he turned and said to Mrs Laden: 'It's a miracle. She is now exactly as she was when I married her. The colour of her hair has gone back to auburn. Her wrinkles have disappeared and her feet look beautiful.' Charlotte did not normally have attractive feet, says Mrs Laden.

Writing later that day to Sidney Webb, whose wife had died a few months earlier, Shaw wrote: 'I also am a widower, Charlotte died this morning at 2.30' – Mrs Laden says it was 12.10. 'Her long illness had changed her greatly, and was very distressing in some ways (she was troubled with hallucinations) but at the end the distresses cleared off; and her last hours were happy.' Similar letters were sent to other of his more intimate friends.

He later went round, that same day, to see John Wardrop, an American, with whom he discussed copyrights, and then, turning to Miss Eleanor O'Connell, an old friend who happened to be in the office, he said: 'Everyone tells me that I am looking well and I can't very well say that it is relief at my wife's death, but it is, you know.' This can, of course, mean that it was relief from the strain of her long illness. But when Lady Astor remarked later how well both he and his secretary, Miss Blanche Patch, were looking, he replied: 'You know, if she had lived much longer we should have pre-deceased her. She completely wore us out.' Asked whether her marriage had made her happy, Shaw said: 'No. She was always discontented, with everything in the world to make her happy, but she had the idea that happiness was always in the place she wished to be or had just left.' Blanche Patch had reservations about Charlotte; she found her possessive and jealous, not only of Shaw's attentions to other women, but also 'of the fact that I had to read and transcribe his shorthand. I knew the text of his latest play before she did' – Shaw always wrote his plays in shorthand. She did not find their love for each other as intense as that of the Webbs – it was just a 'tender affection'. What Miss Patch could never forget was Charlotte's remark about babies. 'Babies,' she exclaimed, 'who could like them? Disgusting little things.'

While talking to Shaw on the day that Charlotte died Eleanor O'Connell asked him if he was sorry they had no children. Without hesitation he put the blame squarely on Charlotte. 'She had a feeling against children,' he said, 'but sometimes I have been sorry that I was not more insistent on that point'; then after a pause he added: 'I don't think I ought to have been married. I am not the marrying sort.'

Shaw and Charlotte often quarrelled, both before and after their marriage. She had a blazing temper, and disagreements, at times on quite trifling subjects, led to an explosion from her, for Shaw kept his temper well under control and spoke always in a quiet voice. But he never withheld his criticisms. He thought her extravagant, though not always spending on herself. 'She was extremely generous,' says Mrs Laden, 'and showered gifts on others. When rebuked, she always answered angrily and at times could be very nasty, not only to him. But after a time she would come up with a smile and apologise most profusely.'

63

In the early months of their acquaintance, to make his criticism more acceptable, Shaw used to split her in his letters into two distinct personalities – this was a favourite device when writing to women. 'I am natural once more,' he wrote. 'You count that I have lost one Charlotte; but I have lost two, and one of the losses is a prodigious relief. . . . Now that she is gone, I realise for the first time the infernal tyranny of the past year, which left me the licence of the rebel, not the freedom of the man who stands alone. I will have no more of it.' He talked of her lying in wait and 'dragging me into bondage, always planning nice, sensible, comfortable, selfish destruction of me'.

Charlotte's passion for travel increased as she got older. She took him to Egypt, South Africa, New Zealand, China, Japan, Hollywood, all over Europe and the United States of America. Shaw grumbled about the pitching and rolling of the ship, found life on board uncomfortable and was always terribly seasick. His only solace while abroad was sightseeing. But Charlotte hated sightseeing. He was also greatly handicapped by his inability to learn languages; with the help of a dictionary he was only just able to read German and French. While in Madeira, after achieving a certain skill in dancing the tango, he decided to follow it up with a course in Spanish. He got Miss Patch to put her name down for a correspondence course and pass the papers on to him. After a few weeks the Director of Instruction criticised Miss Patch for her lack of perseverance. She showed the letter to Shaw and he instantly ordered her to remove her name from the Institute's books.

Charlotte left £154,967. Her will, made six years earlier, bequeathed the bulk of her estate to Shaw for life. Sidney Webb got £1,000; provision was made for various annuities to be paid to the servants, even to those who were no longer in her service; and a substantial sum was bequeathed to her niece Cecily, the daughter of her younger sister Sissy who had married Colonel Cholmondeley. Shaw was in a frantic state at receiving so much money. He wrote to Judy Masters: 'Charlotte left me her separate property valued at £150,000 for my lifetime. The net result is that without being a penny the richer, I have to pay £40,000 to the Govt. and heaven knows what to the lawyers and valuers.' Of course, none of this came out of his own personal estate. He always worried about taxation and could never resist the opportunity of grumbling to all and sundry. To Sidney Webb he wrote: 'Charlotte's death has been a financial disaster for me. During her marriage her property doubled in value, as she quite unintentionally made a profit out of our arrangement by which she paid the housekeeping bills and I paid the rents, the travelling expenses and cars, and gave her £1,200 a year cash. She saved and invested, with the result that whereas she had over £4,000 a year when we married she had £8,000 when she died, and I paid the surtax.

'Now as we lived on our joint incomes my inheritance did not enrich me by a single farthing. But I had to pay £40,000 death duties. Altogether I had to pay considerably more than the £100,000 to the Exchequer since 1939' – that is to say in the four years leading up to her death. 'I have just sold out £30,000 War Loans to clear my personal overdraft; but I (am) still overdrawn heaven knows how much at the National Provincial on Charlotte's account which is a Trust. So much for the popular belief that I am rolling in money as a consequence of having been left £150,000. However, I am on velvet compared to many broken by the war. I am not really insolvent. So enough of this.'

6

Early Struggles as a Dramatist

SHAW'S FIRST PLAY, *Widowers' Houses*, was written in 1885, when he was twenty-nine. He had finished his fifth novel the year before and had begun on his sixth, but, on learning that the fifth too had been rejected by the publishers, he gave up all further thought of becoming a novelist and began to think of writing plays, for in September of that year he had started work as a dramatic critic.

But he was not yet sure of his ability to use this new form. William Archer, the dramatic critic with whom he had established a close friendship, gave him a theme for the play and suggested that Shaw should write the dialogue. The only part of the plot Shaw used was the setting on the Rhine. Archer was furious, and *Widowers' Houses* was set aside for some years while Shaw busied himself with journalistic work. It was not until seven years later, in 1892, that he took the play out again and began to work on it. Some months earlier he had fallen under the spell of Ibsen, about whom Archer, who had translated some of Ibsen's plays into English, had talked most enthusiastically.

Here, Shaw found, was something new in playwriting – there was a purpose and a reforming zeal in Ibsen's plays. Always attracted to what was strikingly different, Shaw decided to expose in his plays the faults in the English social system and to add for good measure the devastating humour he was employing with such brilliant success in his critical articles on music and the theatre. On the London stage at that time, and indeed in the theatres in the provinces, the offering was light romantic comedies in which the audiences saw elegantly dressed men and women exchanging banter over cups of tea in a luxurious drawing-room; romantic costume plays; and very lavish presentations of Shakespeare: all of which delighted the public. They had come for diversion, not to be made to think about social problems. So Ibsen's plays were not acceptable to the managers of the commercial theatre.

Shaw, captivated by Ibsen's method of playwriting, made a close study of his work and thought for a while of writing *Shaw's Tales from Ibsen* on the lines of *Lamb's Tales from Shakespeare*; but he soon decided to write, instead, a book on Ibsen's fierce attacks on accepted conventions. Initially this was written as a lecture and delivered to the Fabian Society in St James's restaurant in July 1890. The following January he extended it and published it under the title *The Quintessence of Ibsenism*; it analysed Ibsen's work, his philosophy and especially the propaganda value of his plays.

It was after this that Shaw had another look at his play *Widowers' Houses* and decided to revise it. Drawing on his experiences as a clerk and a rent-collector in the Dublin estate office, he made the play a powerful indictment of slum landlords. Nobody wanted the play, but J T Grein, who had formed the Independent Theatre for the express purpose of putting on plays on which commercial managers would not risk their money and had already given London Ibsen's *Ghosts*, arranged a production of *Widowers' Houses* in December 1892. The leading rôle of Blanche Sartorius, said to be a portrayal of Jenny Patterson, was played by Florence Farr. Jenny Patterson was in the audience.

The play was hissed and booed by the audience; only the Fabians cheered it. The Press attacked it savagely. His friend William Archer, in the course of his review, advised Shaw not to 'devote further time and energy to a form of production for which he had no real ability'.

After a few nights the play was taken off. Like his novels it had failed, but, unlike them, it had a showing. The vilely abusive criticisms appeared to him to be of small consequence in view of the widespread publicity they had brought him. He wrote *The Philanderer* in the following year (it did not reach the stage until twelve years later); and he then went on to write *Mrs Warren's Profession* about prostitution and a woman who was a brothel-keeper – the censor banned it, but after some years it was put on by the Stage Society for its members. His fourth play *Arms and the Man* was written in 1894, while the others were still hanging fire. This one, however, did get an immediate showing. Miss Horniman, a wealthy woman eager to give the theatre something new, put it on for the general public, and, at considerable cost to herself, kept it going for eleven weeks. The takings averaged a miserable £23 for each performance. Only twice, Shaw says, did the play draw 'as much as half the cost of sending up the curtain'. Once again Florence Farr played the leading rôle. The audience laughed heartily on the first night; there was only one 'boo' and Shaw, taking his bow at the end of the performance, said to the boo-er, 'I quite agree with you, my friend, but what can we two do against all those others?' King Edward VII, then Prince of Wales, went to see it, and after asking who was the author was, added: 'Of course he's mad.'

Advised to adapt himself to the needs of the time and give the public what they want, Shaw's indignant reply was: 'I shall continue writing just as I do now for the next ten years. After that we can wallow in the gold poured at our feet by a dramatically regenerated public.'

But Shaw did in fact make an effort to adjust his style. He studied the needs of the commercial theatre and began to write powerful parts for popular actors and actresses. He also now made comedy his chief ingredient: 'By laughter only,' he said, 'can you destroy evil without malice and affirm good fellowship without mawkishness.' Even melodrama was not overlooked: in 1896 he wrote

The Devil's Disciple for William Terriss, the leading melodramatic actor in England. But Terriss did not like it, so Shaw sent it (since its setting was the American War of Independence) to the popular American actor Richard Mansfield, who put it on in New York in 1897. It proved to be an instantaneous success – Shaw's first – and it brought him about £3,000. It was during the run of this play, after receiving only a part of the money from America, that Shaw married his 'Irish millionairess'.

This was the beginning of a turn in his fortunes. He instantly gave up all his journalistic assignments; even *The Saturday Review*, for which he wrote his dramatic criticisms, was abandoned. Two years later, seeing how successful *The Devil's Disciple* had been in America, Terriss decided to put it on in England, but his assassination at the stage-door of his theatre (the Adelphi in the Strand) put an end to Shaw's hopes. It was presented later at a small theatre in Kennington, in South London. The run was short. Shaw at the time was in Constantinople with his wife; when he returned the play was off.

But Shaw kept on writing – *Candida*, later recognised as one of his great plays; *The Man of Destiny*, which he wrote for Ellen Terry and Henry Irving, though Irving didn't do it; and *You Never Can Tell* which, Shaw confesses, was an attempt to comply with the requirements of managers in search of fashionable comedies for the London theatre. George Alexander couldn't make head or tail of it. Cyril Maude found it too long, and persuaded Shaw to cut it, but even so it wasn't put on.

Disgusted with theatre managers and, in particular, with Henry Irving, whom he had praised in the past, Shaw launched now a succession of ferocious attacks on them. He denounced Irving for his lavish productions of Shakespeare and for doctoring and mutilating the plays instead of using his talent and Ellen Terry's in such modern and realistic plays as Ibsen's. His savage attacks even descended upon Shakespeare – his references to Shakespeare's mental capacity were contemptuous;

Ibsen, he said, was an acute and consistent thinker, whereas Shakespeare was only a spasmodic thinker; and he criticised him particularly for failing to examine the structure of society, which Shakespeare obviously had no wish to do.

Shaw wrote in all fifty-seven plays; the last of them, *Buoyant Billions*, not a good play, was finished in 1948, two years before his death. Of these just over a dozen are outstanding and are often performed now.

Shaw discovered that actor-managers were unable to understand his plays; he felt that only by reading the plays to them himself could the fullest value be given to the correct placing of the emphasis, to the twists in the dialogue, a true significance to the pauses, and an effective springing of the jests, while his gentle Irish lilt supplied a pleasing turn to the romantic passages. That his enunciation was always clear and perfect, and every vowel was given its fullest value, was, of course, an added advantage. But, even so, when Shaw read *The Devil's Disciple* to William Terriss in the flat of his leading actress, Jessie Milward, Terriss, he tells us, fell 'into a coma so profound that Jessie and I had to carry him into the next room and give him some strong tea before he was thoroughly awake'. On another occasion, however, when Winifred Emery, Cyril Maude's wife, refused to play the part of Gloria in *You Never Can Tell*, Shaw's reading of the play was able to prove that Gloria's silence in the early scenes actually made her first speech all the more effective. She was so impressed that before he had finished reading the first act she stretched for a bit of paper and scribbled on it: 'I shall play Gloria.' But Cyril Maude did not put on the play.

Shaw decided then to give the public a chance to read the plays and in the spring of 1898 published seven of them in two volumes under the titles *Plays Unpleasant*, which contained *Widowers' Houses*, *The Philanderer* and *Mrs Warren's Profession*, and *Plays Pleasant*, containing *Arms and the Man*, *Candida*, *The Man of Destiny* and

You Never Can Tell. He abandoned the normal form in which plays had hitherto been printed. The prompt-copy's stage-directions were omitted since only people connected with the theatre could understand them, and instead he gave the reader long, vivid descriptions of each scene and details about each character so that their changing emotions could be carefully observed. The plays had, in consequence, a great deal of the novel in them, and each volume was provided with a preface, in which, with irrelevant autobiographical revelations, Shaw expounded his progressive, and at times revolutionary, views. The Press reviews of these two volumes were for the most part critical, but more and more people got to know of Shaw – many talked of him scoffingly, others with a curiosity which led to an encouraging sale of the books.

In these early days when a play of his went into rehearsal it was impossible to keep Shaw away, but his attempts to interrupt were discouraged and he displayed a distracting restlessness as he sat in the hall and listened. Not until Forbes-Robertson put on *The Devil's Disciple* at the Coronet Theatre, Notting Hill Gate, in 1900, was Shaw, who was required to make certain alterations, actually asked to assist at the rehearsals. He found it more strenuous than he had imagined and complained, unconvincingly, for actually he enjoyed it: 'I am nearly dead with work because of the wiliness of Forbes-Robertson. I usually rely on my bad character to keep me away from rehearsals; but Forbes politely begged me to *conduct* the first rehearsals and settle the business' – meaning the action of the actors – 'besides reading the play. . . . They think that since I only have to prepare one act at a time, it is holiday work for me, whereas with the Vestry, the Fabian, the printers (American and English), and a thousand other things, I am working like mad sixteen hours a day.'

A few years later, early in 1910, Lennox Robinson, the Irish playwright whose *The Whiteheaded Boy* won him a great reputation in 1920, was engaged by Shaw as an additional secretary with a special eye on play production. When Robinson and I were invited by the equivalent of the Arts Council of China to speak at the Shaw centenary celebrations on the 26th July 1956 in Peking, Shanghai and elsewhere in China, Robinson gave me details of his early association with Shaw. 'W B Yeats and Lady Gregory needed a new manager and producer at the Abbey Theatre in Dublin and they thought I ought to have the job. I was in my early twenties at the time and had very little theatrical experience. So they asked Shaw, who was by now a flourishing playwright, if he could do something to help. Shaw complied readily. He sent me a telegram asking me to be his secretary and I left Dublin at once for London. I did no secretarial work at all – I didn't even type a letter.

'As Shaw's secretary I attended all the rehearsals of his new play *Misalliance* at the Duke of York's Theatre. Shaw sat with me in the body of the hall and we talked of the play, the points of emphasis in the dialogue, and about possible adjustments and alterations. I learned a lot from him. He concentrated his attention on the play rather than on those who were playing in it and he insisted that everyone must speak loudly and slowly so that not a word he had written would be missed even by those seated at the back of the gallery. The result was a very slow performance, and after the first night a great deal had to be cut out of *Misalliance*. He had a tremendous talent for getting the utmost out of every word and every action. His love of words and his wit were, of course, essentially Irish, but he had also learned by then to employ all the tricks of the trade as a dramatist.'

On his return to Dublin, Robinson got the job as manager of the Abbey Theatre and was later appointed director of the theatre, retaining the position until his death two years or so after our visit to China. He saw Shaw from time to time – 'generally when I was in London or when Shaw visited our mutual friend Sir

Horace Plunkett in Ireland. Strange as it may seem, I think he was one of the most lovable men I ever met.'

Shaw's rapid recognition in England was due to the opportunity provided him by J E Vedrenne and H Granville-Barker when they decided, in October 1904, to use the Royal Court Theatre in Sloane Square, London, for the presentation of intelligent modern plays which were still frowned on by the commercial theatre managers. *Candida* was performed at half a dozen matinées and was followed by a new Shaw play entitled *John Bull's Other Island*, which had its first performance there on the 1st of November of that year. Later, when the matinées were found to be yielding a modest profit, evening performances were added. In March 1905 the new play was presented at a command performance before King Edward VII who, having once dismissed Shaw as 'mad', chuckled heartily at the rich humour of *John Bull's Other Island*. Another new Shaw play, *Major Barbara*, was staged at the Royal Court later that year and others followed. The turn had come in Shaw's fortunes. *John Bull's Other Island* was performed 121 times, *You Never Can Tell* beat this by having 149 performances, and *Man and Superman* did better still, running to as many as 176 performances.

Shaw attended every rehearsal. After indicating the necessary movements and gestures of the players, he withdrew to the auditorium with his notebook. Not once did he interrupt; he talked to the actors afterwards, supplying the correct vocal inflexions for each part, male and female. He was concerned also with the scenery, going into details of every stage set; the dresses worn by the players – the colour of the clothes and whether they should be fresh, crumpled or torn in the various scenes. Numerous postcards were sent to the director and the players if Shaw thought things were not quite right. Granville-Barker took it very well and they became firm friends. Forty years later, when Shaw was dying, he told Esmé Percy, 'You know Granville-Barker never really understood my plays.' This seemed still to be troubling him.

A master of stagecraft, Shaw knew exactly how every possible effect could be obtained. In a letter to Ronald Gow, the author of the play *Love on the Dole*, in which his wife Wendy Hiller starred (Wendy herself starred later in the film versions of *Pygmalion* and *Major Barbara*), Shaw, writing of a suggested scenario for *Major Barbara*, provided an instructional text for all young dramatic writers. He wrote: 'You must be very careful how you introduce your characters. The star plan is to talk about them before they appear so as to make the audience curious to see them, and sufficiently informed about them to save them the trouble of explaining their circumstance. But as some of the characters must open the play and cannot be prepared in this way, you must either fall back on the Parisian well-made play formula and begin with a conversation between the butler and housemaid or else start the characters with a strongly assertive scene, like *Richard III*.

'In *Barbara* Lady Britomart introduces herself like Richard; but Todger Fairmile (who, by the way, does not appear at all in the play) is introduced very effectively by Shirley and Walker. In your version you have thrown away all the introductions and presented Todger as a nobody.

'You have also quite disregarded building up the interest of the climaxes of the play, cutting it up into little pieces like a jigsaw puzzle, but assuming that it did not matter in what order you put them together again. The havoc you have wrought by this is not to be described. It is not the story that matters but the way it is told. *You* think that it is the story that matters and *not* the way it is told. That delusion will be your ruin if you really entertain it – which you probably don't on reflection.

'The moral is: never work to a ready-made plot unless you are merely manufacturing a detective play. Let the play grow naturally and it will come right. Cut it in bits and force it into a pattern, and you will get nothing but a mechanised abortion.'

Gow, worried about a point of law, was told 'the legalisation in England of marriage with a deceased wife's sister or husband's brother was quite recent and did not exist at Cusins's birth. It knocked *Barbara* out of date; but it also knocked out *Hamlet.*

'It is no use trying to shift the interest of a play to adapt it to a lower class of audience. The result is neither the one thing nor the other: it is spoiled for both audiences. And of all such attempts the most hopeless is to de-Shavianise and Hollywoodise a Shavian play. Barbara and Cusins will not do as Mary and Daisy.

'Tell Wendy to make them dress the sister as brilliantly as possible, as Barbara has to get her effect by running *against* her. The secret of effective dressing, as Ellen Terry knew, was never to be in the fashion: that is, like anybody else, but always like nobody on earth. Excuse this scrawl – G Bernard Shaw.'

During these years, and indeed ever since his marriage, the social side of his life was admirably catered for by Charlotte. There were regular luncheon parties at 10 Adelphi Terrace and later at Whitehall Court to which H G Wells, Bertrand Russell, Sean O'Casey, Sybil Thorndike, Lewis Casson, Rebecca West and other famous writers, actors and actresses, politicians and economists were invited; incidentally at these lunches meat and fish were served as well as wine, of all of which Charlotte partook. Cigarettes were passed round and in this too Charlotte joined the guests. Bertrand Russell talked to me of these occasions. 'Inconceivable as it may seem, I found Shaw an awful bore. He took an absolute delight in talking about his relatives on his father's side and summed them up as being totally mad. Amusing the first time one heard them, they became painful when repeated, as they were at every meal, and Charlotte, out of consideration for those who were unfortunate enough to be seated near him, used to move us to her end of the table, but his voice carried and we heard the same stories again and again. There was his father's brother, William, for example, whose chief diversion was to sit on the beach at Dalkey with a bible on his knees and a pair of opera glasses to his eyes watching the women coming out of the sea. In the end Uncle William was removed to an asylum where he committed suicide by sticking his head into a carpet bag and shutting it. He was probably trying to decapitate or strangle himself, but in fact he died of heart failure.'

Sean O'Casey found Charlotte very trying at these lunches. She 'ate heavily, a great pile on her plate', and, feeling the cold keenly, sat hunched up over her food, a shawl around her shoulders and an electric fire beside her chair. And she would direct sharp criticisms at O'Casey during the meal. Asking him what he was doing now, when told 'nothing at the moment', she turned on him. 'Too busy quarrelling,' she said, rather viciously, he records in *Sunset and Evening Star*. 'I hear you have quarrelled with Agate now. You will have to learn a better way of conducting yourself. You will get nowhere with these senseless disputes.' The guests were 'mostly Mrs Shaw's cronies', he notes, and Shaw was plagued to give his opinions on persons and things past and gone, by those who had come with pick and spade to disinter them and make them look lively again. Shaw said he found it a great strain to keep talking through lunch. 'Why the hell do you do it?' O'Casey asked. 'Is it vanity, is it just trying to shine?' to which Shaw replied: 'They all expect it of me. One can't sit in silence, staring at the others.' Augustus John, on the other hand, O'Casey noticed, talked only when he felt like it.

Shortly after her engagement to Ronald Gow, Wendy Hiller and her fiancé were asked to lunch at Whitehall Court. Shaw placed her alongside a young, very good-looking man, well connected and rich. The meal had barely begun when he turned to her and said: 'I have put you there, Wendy, so that before you marry you will have the chance of considering whether you have chosen the right man. The one I have put beside you is a good catch. He has money and fine looks. Don't you think it would be a much better match than marrying Ronald?' Wendy smiled with embarrassment, regarding it as a joke, but the jest was less pleasing to her fiancé. She married Ronald nevertheless shortly afterwards.

Wee Georgie Wood, the music-hall entertainer who has been on the stage since he was a child, was often at the Shaw lunches. GBS used to take him aside before the meal and say: 'Now don't forget. When we've finished eating but before we leave the table I want you to sing 'Chick-chick-chick-chick-chicken'. Don't say a word about it to anyone because I want to do the crowing.'

'This happened every time I was there,' Wee Georgie Wood told me. 'I would start with "Chick-chick-chick-chick-chicken, will you lay a little egg for me" and when the egg was laid, Shaw would raise his head and his beard and most triumphantly cry out "Cock-a-doodle do!" '

7

My First Contacts with Shaw

MY FIRST CONTACT with Bernard Shaw was made by letter. A very young journalist at the time, I wrote to tell him that the daily newspaper *The Englishman*, on which I worked in Calcutta, was about to celebrate its centenary, and I asked if he would send us a message to mark the occasion. Many exalted men – former viceroys, commanders-in-chief, governors, numerous statesmen, both English and Indian, writers, artists and others – had responded readily, eager to commend the long unbroken record of the oldest English journal other than *The Times* and *The Morning Post* of London. Shaw's reply, written in his neat handwriting, every word clearly legible as though it was being enunciated by him, came on a pale blue postcard. Dated the 20th September 1920, its content was acid. 'I am not a writer of greetings, but of serious articles on serious occasions; and I have no time to undertake any extra work at present; but of course I am always open to a business proposal as a matter of professional routine. But if newspapers cannot celebrate their centenaries and birthdays and Christmases and New Years without help from me, they must perish. My own opinion is that these greetings and messages and so forth bore the reader horribly, as they certainly do the writer – G Bernard Shaw.'

The newspaper, unable to pay, had to forgo his blessing. It managed to survive, but not for very long. It was swallowed up by its competitor, five years later, and so perished – for all he cared!

A later attempt to interview him was side-tracked on

the same pretext: no money, no interview. Not long afterwards, as acting editor of *The Sunday News* in London, I found myself in a position to pay for his contribution. The evening papers had printed an attack on boxing by Hall Caine and I felt that Shaw, as author of *Cashel Byron's Profession*, was best qualified to reply. I telephoned his London flat in Whitehall Court and he answered the phone himself. Told of Hall Caine's attack, he enquired 'Who?' and on my repeating the name, Shaw said: 'He's the man who gets himself up to look like Shakespeare. I shall be delighted to dispose of him and his silly arguments.' He asked where the attack had appeared. I told him. 'Now, young man,' he said, 'we come to the important question. How much are you going to pay me?'

'How much would you want for an article running to about one thousand words?' I asked.

'I want a million pounds,' he replied.

I laughed – a little nervously.

'It is no laughing matter,' he said sharply. 'That's my price.' Then, adjusting his voice to a pleasing Irish lilt, he added: 'But as you appear to be a nice young man, very new to all this, I'll tell you what I'm prepared to take from you. I'll make it half a million pounds.'

'You are not serious, Mr Shaw?'

'Indeed I'm very serious.'

'You no doubt know this newspaper,' I said, 'and you will have seen how small our advertising revenue is. We are struggling to pay our way. I would very much like to have your article.'

'How much can you give me?' he asked. I was silent, realising that the figure we could afford would dash all my hopes of getting the article.

'How much?' he repeated.

'I hesitate to tell you, Mr Shaw. I'm afraid if I tell you what we can afford your answer will be a scornful "No". Will you be so kind as to write the article and let me have it by Friday morning – and could you leave it to me to send you a bigger cheque than we normally send our contributors?'

'I can't agree to that,' he said.

'Oh!' I couldn't think of anything more to say.

I apologised for bothering him and thanked him for entertaining a proposition which unfortunately could not be fulfilled on my side. Then we both hung up.

Three days later, on the Friday morning, his article arrived – a scintillating, witty and scathing attack on the man who went about with a small beard like Shakespeare's. Boxing was most vigorously defended and justified as a great sport.

The article attracted considerable attention. Letters poured in with arguments for and against. I sent Shaw a cheque for twenty-five guineas and he accepted it. His generosity helped very substantially one of the lesser Sunday newspapers and, of course, redounded very much to my personal credit for pulling off what appeared to be a scoop.

In the years that followed I had quite a number of articles from Shaw. Always approachable and often on the phone himself, he was prepared to write on almost any subject. Money was never discussed again, he left it to me to pay what I could, unlike H G Wells, who always specified the price he wanted, invariably two or three times as high as what I could pay Shaw. 'Take it or leave it,' Wells would say. 'Don't haggle.' Once, for a short article of only 150 words which I wanted for the *Strand Magazine*, Wells exclaimed: 'Tiny contribution indeed! The gist of a life's experience for £10! I like your cheek. It will take me hours to compose the brief message' – yet he wrote it on what was left of the sheet of notepaper.

In his later years, when I phoned Shaw to discuss a contribution, he would say: 'Young man, look at the calendar, I am too old, much too old.' Even so, I was occasionally able to break down his resistance and he wrote it or sent me an answer to a questionnaire.

Meetings occurred from time to time, both when I

(Above left) Shaw in January 1925, aged sixty-nine. *(Above right)* Shaw, in his thirties – a typically militant pose taken about 1890. He gave the photograph *(right)* to Alice Laden, for many years his devoted housekeeper, and wrote on the back of it, 'When this old hat was new, so was I'. He was then in his 94th year. *(Radio Times Hulton Picture Library)*.

1905 – Mr and Mrs Shaw, relaxing at home.
(*Right*): Mrs Stella Patrick Campbell – 'O Stella Stellarum' to Shaw throughout their twenty-eight years of close but stormy friendship that ended with her death in 1940. *(Radio Times Hulton Picture Library).*

was a journalist and later when I went into the film world where I worked as a writer and a producer. When his play *Caesar and Cleopatra* was being filmed, with Vivien Leigh, Claude Rains, Stewart Granger and Michael Rennie in the leading rôles, Gabriel Pascal, the producer, phoned to ask me for the loan of Granger and Rennie, who were busy on a film I was making. It was not easy to adjust my schedule. Each of them was booked to appear in scenes with other artists on the days Pascal wanted them. After much rearranging and complicated adjustments – revisions of this kind were always costly – I managed to release Granger and Rennie on the dates Pascal had given me.

I had no personal contact with Shaw over this, all the arrangements were made by Pascal. But about four years later, when Shaw was dying, he recalled what had been done and asked if I would go to see him. The invitation was for tea. A day or two after I received his invitation Shaw fell in his garden and had to be taken to hospital. When he returned home, the invitation was repeated and a date was fixed – Friday, the 27th October 1950.

As the day approached it became increasingly obvious to me that it would not be possible for him to receive and entertain me. I waited until the morning on which I was due to go to 'Shaw's Corner' and telephoned Mrs Laden. When I gave her my name, she said: 'Mr Shaw is expecting you at four o'clock.'

'How is Mr Shaw?' I asked.

'He's in bed,' she said. 'We've moved his bed down into the dining-room.'

'Don't you think it would be better if I didn't come, seeing how ill he is?'

'Mr Shaw especially mentioned this morning, 'It's today Mr Minney is coming, isn't it?' He said he was looking forward to seeing you, so I hope you *will* come.'

Accompanied by Percy Dayton, the film technician who had brought me Shaw's invitation, I drove to

'Shaw's Corner'. When we arrived we found the gates shut and a large number of pressmen with cameras waiting in the street outside. I opened the gates and we drove in. The doorbell was answered by Maggie, the young Irish maid, who said briefly: 'Mr Shaw is unable to receive any visitors,' and quickly shut the door.

I pressed the bell a second time and asked Maggie if I could see Mrs Laden, but was told that she was out.

'Will you tell her when she returns that I'd be glad to see her.' I gave her my name and returned to the car to wait.

After a while Mrs Laden came to the front door and called to me. 'Mr Shaw is asleep,' she said as she took us into the long, narrow drawing-room dotted with busts of Shaw. 'I'll bring you some tea,' she added, 'and I will let you know when he's awake. He'll be muzzy at first and we shall have to allow about twenty minutes before you can go in to see him.'

Tea, bread-and-butter and some cake were brought for us. I wandered round the cluttered Victorian room as the gathering darkness blotted out the autumn greyness of the garden. Books choked the shelves and almost tumbled out of the revolving bookcase – books on history political economy and many biographies, most of them inscribed by the authors. On the mantelpiece, laden with assorted Chelsea cottages and other china ornaments, was the tall golden Oscar awarded to Shaw for his screen-play of *Pygmalion*. On the wall hung a most charming portrait of Charlotte, painted by Sartorio some years before Shaw had met her and originally intended as a gift for Axel Munthe.

Slowly the door of the room opened and I saw Mrs Laden standing there. 'You can go in now. But you mustn't stay more than four minutes.'

The dining-room was alongside and the door to it was slightly ajar. There was not much room between it and the steep flight of stairs leading up to his old bedroom on the first floor.

We went into the small narrow room. The bed had three wooden slats as its headboard. The great man, his complexion pink-and-white like a baby's, had very few strands left of his beard. But his hair and eyebrows had their normal white abundance and his eyes were, as always, a bright penetrating blue. His feet stretched towards the window, but the counterpane was so flat that there seemed to be nothing under it, not even a hint of his body or his very long legs.

His eyes were turned fixedly, first on me, then on Dayton. He did not appear to recognise either of us. I noticed two parchment scrolls flowing down from the headboard, one on each side of him and stretching over his shoulders right down to the foot of the bed. I was told later that they had been given to him when he received the Freedom of Dublin and the Freedom of the Borough of St Pancras. He had insisted that they should be placed there so that he might die wearing this strange insignia.

I glanced at the mantelpiece on the further side of the bed. On it I saw photographs of Gandhi, of Lenin and Stalin.

Shaw, still wondering who I was, said at last: 'Well? What do you want?' It was a puzzled enquiry and I got the feeling that he may have imagined we had been sent by the undertaker to measure him for his coffin.

I told him my name, and a slight smile lit up his eyes and played gently round his thin lips. 'Oh yes,' he said. 'I wanted to see you to thank you personally for being so kind as to let us have two stars from your film for the making of my last film, *Caesar and Cleopatra*.'

'I was glad to be able to arrange it,' I said.

'It helped. We could not have got on without them.' It seemed odd that he should remember this after four years.

His voice had its normal briskness. There was not the slightest sign of a quiver in it. Each word was, as always, pronounced distinctly. Scarcely any difference would have been detected in it if one compared it with a recording of the voice I had heard for the first time more than twenty years before.

'Did you see the film?' he asked.

'Yes,' I said.

'Did you like it?' he enquired in a voice that was sharp and peremptory.

I had not liked all of it. To say so would have involved a careful analysis of the direction and the acting, and Mrs Laden had not allowed me enough time for that.

I said: 'I preferred some of your other films.'

'Which others?' His gaze had hardened. His voice was not quite so soft and gentle.

'*Pygmalion*, for instance,' I replied.

'Why?'

'I thought it was brilliantly directed by Anthony Asquith, and extremely well acted. Leslie Howard and Wendy Hiller were excellent. . . .'

He shook his head more violently than I had expected. 'It was not a good film,' he said with surprising emphasis, the emphasis he would have brought to a public debate in the old days.

'Why do you say that?' I enquired.

'Leslie Howard was not right – not at all right. I said so, but they would not listen to me.'

'I thought he played Higgins admirably.'

'He could not have bent Eliza to his will, man,' he said sharply. 'He couldn't have done it. He did not possess the strength of will, the strength of purpose to mould her.'

'Who did you have in mind for the rôle?'

'Charles Laughton. He would have been the perfect Higgins.'

I considered this. Laughton certainly would have been a hard enough task-master, with the harshness and savagery of a bully – he would doubtless have brought power and greater strength to the performance. 'But,' I said, 'you would have lost all the tenderness Leslie Howard supplied.'

84

He shook his head vigorously. 'It was not a tender part. It was *not* a love story.' His eyes were very stern now.

I said nothing. There was silence for a moment. Then he said: 'You know I got an Oscar for writing the film script?'

'I saw it on the mantelpiece in the next room.'

He stared at me, then, astonishingly, he asked: 'Do you think it's gold?'

I smiled.

'It's quite heavy, you know,' he went on. 'Pick it up – pick it up when you get back to the room. I'd like to know.'

Once again I smiled, casting doubts on his hopes. He didn't appear to like that, but he pursued it no further.

Changing the subject, he talked of Gabriel Pascal, the Hungarian producer, who had descended without an appointment on Shaw in his flat at Whitehall Court in the spring of 1935.

Blanche Patch, Shaw's austere secretary, answered the door and doubted if Shaw would see him. Pascal told her he had a taxi waiting and there was already a few shillings on the clock. Feeling sorry for the squat, tubby Hungarian with dark glittering eyes, a massive head of black hair and a persuasive charm in his accent, she left him at the door and went into the study, knowing that Shaw was always partial to foreigners. He was struck by her description of the man, and Pascal, before being ushered into the forbidding presence, fumbled in his pocket for the few shillings he possessed and asked if she would be kind enough to pay off his taxi.

Pascal's adulatory approach made a tremendous impression on Shaw. He wanted, he said, to film most if not all of Shaw's plays. This was not the first approach Shaw had had. A number of film companies, American and European, had tried to obtain the great man's consent, but he was adamant about not allowing one word of the text to be cut. Pascal's approach was different.

He was prepared to use the entire stage-play without any alteration whatsoever. That got him over the first hurdle. There was another still to be surmounted. All the other film companies had insisted on the normal practice that the film rights should be bought outright. Shaw for his part refused to depart from his claim to royalties or a percentage of the profits. To this, too, Pascal agreed and a contract was signed for the filming of *Pygmalion*. A year or so later *Major Barbara* was filmed; and then *Caesar and Cleopatra*.

Lying on his deathbed, Shaw talked now of Pascal, and I noticed a sadness fill his eyes. 'Gabriel has not been to see me,' he said in a hurt voice.

'He's abroad, you know,' I explained.

'Abroad? Where?'

'I hear he's in Rome.'

'Rome,' he repeated softly. His expression was reflective. 'I read in the newspapers,' he said, 'that he had gone to India' – the word was separated into three distinct syllables – 'to try to raise money from the Ma-ha-ra-jahs for my next film. Then I read that he had gone to Hollywood to arrange the filming of one of my plays there. Now you say he's in Rome.' Then with a twinkle he added: 'That's the trouble with the man. Rome, Roam, Roam. All over the place.'

It was unworthy of him, though puns of this kind have crept into his plays occasionally. I felt he was getting tired, for his voice was very low now and marked with a very broad Irish brogue. I thought of taking my leave. Becoming aware of this, he said: 'When you two bhoys go through that door, you will say, "The old blighter's dying." '

'We'll say nothing of the kind,' I replied. 'We hope you will get well soon.'

The vigour returned instantly to his voice. He shook his head violently and speaking with great emphasis barked: 'For God's sake don't say that to me. I don't want to live. I want to die. I have *nothing* to live for.'

Percy Dayton, speaking for the first time, said: 'You have your work, sir.'

'My work is finished. I am ninety-five now' – it was not quite accurate: he was just three months over ninety-four. 'A man of worth, he's had his day, now let him go.'

It sounded like a quotation, which I have not been able to trace, even in his own plays. Possibly it was from a play that had been taking shape in his mind.

'You have your memories,' Percy said.

Again he shook his head with startling vigour. 'They are awful memories – *horrible* memories.' He shut his eyes to blot them out.

It was time for us to go. We had stayed far beyond the allotted four minutes.

'Goodbye, sir,' I said.

He held out a limp hand, quite unlike his usual firm grip. It was thrust towards me with a quick jerk and then towards Percy. 'Goodbye . . . goodbye . . . goodbye . . .' he kept saying, like a gramophone of which the needle had got stuck. And it went on, growing fainter and fainter as we walked out of the room.

Mrs Laden, waiting at the door, led us back to the drawing-room. 'You've been there a long time,' she said. 'How do you find him?'

'Surprisingly vigorous,' I said.

'The doctor said he could live for some years if he wanted to. But he doesn't. Just another small operation – not difficult or dangerous. But Mr Shaw refuses to have it. He keeps saying he wants to die.'

I looked sadly round the drawing-room and then went into his study at the foot of the stairs – it was too cold to go out to the hut at the end of the garden. By his typewriter in the study I saw the Bible he always kept there, and on the wall, just at his elbow, was a photograph of the interior of Dublin Cathedral.

'Has this got any significance?' I asked Mrs Laden.

'Yes. Here, just under the stone floor – at this spot

in the foreground – Mr Shaw has always said he wants to be buried.'

I wondered if he had changed his mind, for when his wife died it was arranged, as had been agreed by them, that their ashes should be mingled and scattered in the garden at Ayot St Lawrence.

Shaw died five days later, in the early morning of 2nd November.

8
Shaw and Religion

SHAW USED TO insist that he was an atheist, by which he
meant that he did not believe that there was a God. But
despite this repeated assertion, there is no doubt that he
was a deeply religious man. A reconciliation of sorts was
achieved by giving God the new name of Life Force. He
did not apparently believe that you could pray to the
Life Force, nor was his a mystical religion like Charlotte's,
the interpretation of which she had always been seeking
and never really found. Insistently he proclaimed himself
to be a Protestant, and dissociated himself completely
from the Roman Catholic form of Christianity. We have
already noted how deeply he resented being sent
by his mother's music-teacher, George Vandaleur Lee,
to a Catholic school which he left after six months to
return to a Protestant school.

His mother, born a Protestant like his father, had
declared herself to be an atheist when Shaw was a child.
Yet the family used to go to church regularly until Shaw
was ten years old. By then Shaw had developed a great
affection for the Bible and read it, he tells us, 'straight
through', thus acquiring a knowledge that brought him
to the top of his class in school; this was not his normal
grading in any of the other subjects. His attachment to
the Bible was life-long. One copy was kept on his desk,
another, known as 'My Travelling Bible', he always took
with him wherever he went. 'If he went to London from
Ayot St Lawrence,' Mrs Laden told me, 'he took that
Bible with him. When we first settled down in the country
shortly after Mrs Shaw's death and he set out on his

usual evening walk through the village, I was often worried when he was late in returning home. He was eighty-six years old then and I used to wonder if he had fallen and injured himself – and I went out into the streets to look for him. At the post-office, where he often called to talk to the postmistress, Mrs Lyth, and at other places, I asked anxiously after him. I was told that they had seen him but did not know where he was. One day when he had been missing for more than two hours, I was quite frantic. I enquired at every cottage, even at the pub, The Brocket Arms, although I knew Mr Shaw could not possibly be in there as he was a teetotaller. In the end, in desperation, I went into the church and there to my surprise I found him sitting in one of the pews deep in meditation. I never worried after that, for that's where I always found him when he was out too long. I discovered that he used to go into the church quite often in the evenings just to sit there. I wondered what he thought about, for he used to pretend that he did not believe in God. But what would he be doing in a church if he had no religion?'

As far back as January 1896, when Shaw was not yet forty, he wrote an article entitled 'On Going to Church' for *The Savoy* magazine. In it he wrote: 'I have myself tried the experiment of not eating meat or drinking tea, coffee or spirits for more than a dozen years past, without, as far as I can discover, placing myself at more than my natural disadvantages relatively to those colleagues of mine who patronise the slaughter-house and the distillery. But then I go to Church. If you should chance to see, in a country churchyard, a bicycle leaning against a tombstone, you are not unlikely to find me inside the church if it is old enough or new enough to be fit for its purpose. There I find rest without langour and recreation without excitement, both of a quality unknown to the traveller who turns from the village church to the village inn and seeks to renew himself with shandygaff.' He dismisses certain 'respectable-looking' church interiors which lack the 'Omnipresence, since the bishop's blessing is no spell of black magic to imprison Omnipotence in a place that must needs be intolerable to Omniscience'. During his travels abroad he found 'The innumerable daily services' disturbing to 'the truly religious visitor. If these were decently and intelligently conducted by genuine mystics to whom the Mass was no mere rite or miracle, but a real Communion, the celebrants might reasonably claim a place in the church as their share of the common human right to use it.'

Essentially Shaw was a thinker, and though most of the thoughts he expressed about life were a topsy turvy but witty adjustment of the accepted conventions, which appealed inevitably to the emergent generations and were accepted by them as Holy writ, his thoughts often dwelt too on religion, on the mystery of life and death and on the hereafter, if any.

In his preface, written when he was at last able to publish his very first novel *Immaturity* in 1921, he says: 'My conception of God was that insisted on in the first Article of the Church of England, then as now vehemently repudiated by all pious persons, who will have it that God is a substantial gentleman of uncertain and occasionally savage temper, and a spirit only in the sense in which an archbishop is a spirit'; and he adds: 'It seems providential that I was driven to the essentials of religion by the reduction of every factitious or fictitious element in it to the most irreverent absurdity.'

Dr William Maxwell, managing director of the famous printers R & R Clark, of Edinburgh, who printed all Shaw's works from 1898 until 1950, was a close friend of his during those fifty-two years. He insists that Shaw was a believer in God and in immortality. To support this he draws attention to the conversation between the brothers Barnabas in *Back to Methuselah*, in which one brother says to the other that man is not God's last word; and that God may in His Almighty power wipe man out altogether if man fails to carry out His purpose, and may create a new race that is able to do so. In Lilith's closing speech in the same play Shaw makes her say: 'Of life only there is no end; and though of its million starry mansions many are empty, and still unbuilt, and though its vast domain is as yet unbearably desert, my seed shall one day fill it and master its matter to its uttermost confines. And for what may be beyond, the eyesight of Lilith is too short. It is enough that there is a beyond.'

One could keep on quoting from Shaw's other plays and books: 'Government is impossible without a religion' (*Androcles and the Lion*); 'Every Church should be a Church of All Saints, and every cathedral a place for pure contemplation by the greatest minds of all races, creeds and colours' (*Everybody's Political What's What*); and 'And now look at me and behold the supreme tragedy of the atheist who has lost his faith – his faith in atheism, for which more martyrs have perished than for all the creeds put together' (*Too True to be Good*).

Dame Sybil Thorndike, who first met Shaw in 1908 and saw him from time to time until his death (he wrote *St Joan* for her and she appeared also in a number of his other plays), insists that Shaw was a deeply religious man. The daughter of Canon Thorndike, she reads the Bible every day and uses a photograph of Shaw as a bookmark. She told me:

'GBS often talked about religion to me. Nothing abstruse or analytical – perhaps because I am not clever; but he had read a lot about it and constantly thought about it. He seemed to know the Bible almost by heart and was always quoting from it.

'His deep interest in religion is apparent, of course, in *St Joan*, and it is also apparent in most of his other plays. In conversation he was apt to be reserved about his feelings on religion. He regarded it as something private. We must remember that essentially he was a very shy man and so he was always very reserved about his personal beliefs. He said once: "I would be a Catholic if they would accept a freethinker." It seems to me that what he meant by it was this: "I am a Christian though it may be difficult to classify me as one because I disregard the existing frontiers and adjust the existing tenets to make them acceptable to my way of thinking and my own personal beliefs." '

She then spoke of Shaw's long and close friendship with Dame Laurentia McLachlan, the Abbess of Stanbrook, the Benedictine Abbey just outside Worcester. 'It was through Sir Sydney Cockerell, an old friend of Shaw's who had accompanied him on the early Workers Guild tours in Italy, that GBS met Dame Laurentia. When Cockerell suggested the meeting, the Abbess replied: "I have never heard of Mr Bernard Shaw." Nevertheless Shaw's wife wrote to the Abbess and on the next day called at the abbey with GBS. It was a long and happy friendship, in many ways most revealing of Shaw's true feelings about religion.

'When Lewis and I' – Sybil Thorndike was referring to her husband, Sir Lewis Casson – 'stayed with the nuns, Dame Laurentia talked often of GBS. There is a most fascinating account of their association in the tribute paid to Dame Laurentia after her death by the Benedictines of Stanbrook.'

Born Margaret McLachlan at Coatbridge in Lanarkshire, in 1866, which made her ten years younger than Shaw, Dame Laurentia was the daughter of a handsome, witty Highlander and became a novice at Stanbrook in 1884 when she was eighteen. Forty-one years later, in 1925, she was appointed Prioress and did not become the Abbess until 1931, when she was sixty-five. Thus at the time of her first meeting with Shaw in 1924 she was only a sub-Prioress. *St Joan* had its first production on the 26th March 1924 at the New Theatre with Sybil Thorndike in the title-rôle. The play was hailed as a masterpiece by both Catholics and Protestants. A copy of the play was sent by Cockerell to Dame Laurentia and when the Shaws called to see her they were able to discuss it. Writing to Cockerell after the meeting, Dame

Laurentia described the conversation as 'very pleasant'. But Shaw's report to Cockerell was much more enthusiastic. Asked when he would be going to see her again, he replied, 'Never,' but changed his mind shortly afterwards and added: 'I'll go whenever I can.' Told of this, Dame Laurentia wrote a note which she put away among her private papers. It stated: 'This gives me confidence to hope that God may use me for this soul's salvation. If it were only a matter of his liking me I should think little of it, but it seems that the life here, and therefore the Church, does attract him. God, give me grace to help this poor wanderer so richly endowed by you.'

He visited her for the second time six weeks later and sent her a copy of *St Joan*, published in book form with a preface; it was inscribed 'To Sister Laurentia from Brother Bernard'.With much of the preface she was able to agree; he referred to Joan's visions of saints and angels, clothed in rich garments and visible to the eye in bodies which they did not really possess; they were symbols in accord with the ideas of the person who sees them or of the painters of that period. 'Visionaries are neither impostors nor lunatics. It is one thing to say that the figure Joan recognised as St Catherine was not really St Catherine, but the dramatisation, by Joan's imagination, of that pressure upon her of the driving force that is behind evolution. . . . The simplest French peasant, who believes in apparitions of celestial personages to favoured mortals, is nearer to the scientific truth about Joan than the Rationalist and Materialist historians and essayists who feel obliged to set down a girl who saw saints and heard them talking to her, as either crazy or mendacious. . . . When in the case of exceptionally imaginative persons, especially those practising certain appropriate austerities, the hallucination extends from the mind's eye to the body's, the visionary sees Khrishna or the Buddha or the Blessed Virgin or St Catherine as the case may be. . . . Let us then once for all drop all nonsense about Joan being cracked, and accept her as at least as sane as Florence Nightingale, who also combined a very simple iconography of religious belief with a mind so exceptionally powerful that it kept her in continual trouble with the medical and military panjandrums of her time.'

Dame Laurentia rejected his remark that Catholicism deters freethinkers from joining it because the Catholic Church has no place for them. She challenged him to define what he meant by freethought and added that she suspected that his freethought was synonymous with false thought, since truth alone makes a man free. But it was not over that that they quarrelled. The quarrel came seven years later when Shaw wrote his book *The Adventures of the Black Girl in Her Search for God*. The shock of this book was all the greater on Dame Laurentia because it followed only a few months after Shaw's rapturous letters to her from the Holy Land. But let us deal with that first.

Early in 1931, he set out from England together with his wife and Dean Inge, the Dean of St Paul's Cathedral in London. His letters, some of which were accompanied by snapshots taken by him and like most of his pictures not too well focussed, were long (one of them ran to thirteen sheets), full of vivid details, sensitive, sincere and imbued with an extraordinary feeling for Christian tradition. One is tempted to quote the whole of it, but a few extracts will suffice to show the depth of the impression the scenes made on him.

'You find yourself in the Holy Land by night, with strange new constellations all over the sky and the old ones topsy turvy, but with the stars soft and large and down quite close overhead in a sky which you feel to be of a deep and lovely blue. When the light comes you have left the land of Egypt with its endlessly flat Delta, and are in a hilly country, with patches of cultivation wrested from the omnipresent stones. Here you instantly recognise with a strange emotion which increases when you see a small boy coming down one of the patches, and

95

presently, when he has passed, a bigger lad of about thirteen, beginning to think, and at last, when he too has vanished, a young man, very grave and somewhat troubled, all three being dressed just as Christ dressed.... The appearance of a woman with an infant in her arms takes on the quality of a vision. It gives you the feeling that here Christ lived and grew up, and that here Mary bore him and reared him, and that there is no land on earth quite like it.'

Then further in the same letter, after saying: 'You asked me for a relic from Calvary,' Shaw goes on: 'So off I went to Bethlehem, a beautifully situated hill-town; and from the threshold of the Church of the Nativity I picked up a stone, a scrap of the limestone rock which certainly existed when the feet of Jesus pattered about on it and the feet of Mary pursued him to keep him in order; for he was a most inconsiderate boy where his family was concerned as you would realise if you travelled over the distance (at least a day's journey without a Rolls-Royce) his mother had to go back to look for him when he gave her the slip to stay and argue with the doctors of divinity. In fact I picked up two little stones: one to be thrown blindfold among the others in the Stanbrook garden so that there may always be a stone from Bethlehem there, though nobody will know which it is and be tempted to steal it, and the other for your own self. You will have them when I return, unless I perish on the way, in which case I shall present myself at the heavenly gate with a stone in each hand, and St Peter will stand at attention and salute the stones (incidentally saluting *me* when he has unlocked the gate and flung it open before me). At least he would if it were ever locked which I don't believe.'

He concludes his letter with these words: 'The man who wrote the Book of Revelations, who was *not* the John of the fourth gospel (the Dean assures me that his Greek was disgracefully ungrammatical), ought to have married St Helena. I *know* he was a drug addict, as all

(Above) July 1934 – GBS with two of the players at rehearsals of his *Androcles and the Lion* in the open-air theatre, Regent's Park *(Radio Times Hulton Picture Library)*. (Below) Greer Garson visits GBS at Ayot St Lawrence.

(Right) One of Shaw's
letters to Mrs Patrick
Campbell, shown here on
a reconstruction of her
make-up table at the
Royalty Theatre *(Radio
Times Hulton Picture
Library). (Below)* Lenin
and Stalin kept GBS
company on the mantel-
piece at 'Shaw's Corner'.

the wickednesses of which he accuses God, all the imaginary horrors, all the passings of a thousand years in a second and the visions of universes breaking into three pieces, are the regular symptoms of drug addiction and delirium tremens. The book is a disgrace to the Bible and should never have been admitted to the canon.'

Dame Laurentia was delighted with the letter. She noted: 'Brother Bernard's is a splendid document, the least merit being its brilliancy. I believe his criticisms are such as I should have made myself if I had been there. . . . The tenderness of some passages is beautiful and reveals, I imagine, the soul of the real GBS.'

On the 12th June he sent her one of the two stones. 'This is for the garden. Your particular one will come later.' He took that to her personally. The stone had been exquisitely mounted in silver in the pattern of a mediaeval reliquary, with a chalice-like base decorated with vine leaves alternating with bunches of grapes and surmounted by a conical canopy supported by four slender columns; above this was a haloed figure of the child Jesus, His left hand supporting the globe, His right hand raised in a blessing. In the midst of this elaborate and most attractive mounting, which was almost a foot in height, was the stone from Bethlehem, a piece of rock, irregular in shape and barely an inch across. Dame Laurentia was enchanted with the gift. She wrote later to ask if he would supply an appropriate inscription to be placed on it. He replied with characteristic bluntness: 'Why can it not be a secret between us and Our Lady and her little boy? What the devil – saving your cloth – could be put on it?. . . We couldn't put our names on it – could we? . . . Dear Sister: our finger-prints are on it, and Heaven knows whose footprints may be on the stone. Isn't that enough?' In a PS he added: 'Let the sisters give me all the prayers they can spare; and don't forget me in yours.' This seems to suggest that he did believe in prayer.

In the roving life Shaw was drawn into living since his marriage, that particular year, 1931, had taken him to Egypt and the Holy Land, then to Russia; and before the year ended he was in South Africa – though not all of it was of Charlotte's contriving; she did not in fact accompany him to Russia. She did, however, take him to South Africa and it was there, while she was recovering from a motor accident for which he was responsible, that Shaw wrote *The Adventures of the Black Girl in Her Search for God.* He was such an ignorant and careless driver that it was not unusual for a journey to end in an accident whether he was on a bicycle or in a car. Driving at great speed along the road at Knysna in Cape Province he put his foot on the accelerator instead of the brake, turned abruptly to the left instead of the right, leapt up a bank, tore through some barbed wire and came to a stop only when Commander Newton, who was seated beside him, told him to take his foot off the accelerator. He found his wife, who was in the back seat, buried under the great pile of luggage. She was seriously injured. Shaw describes her condition in a letter to Lady Astor: 'Her head was broken, her spectacle rims were driven into her blackened eyes, her left wrist was agonisingly sprained; her back was fearfully bruised; and she had a hole in her right shin which something had pierced to the bone.' Her temperature, the doctors found, was 108. Shaw and the Commander were unhurt.

It was during the long weeks of her slow recovery that Shaw wrote the *Black Girl.* It runs to 17,000 words. Regarded as a fable, the book had a wide sale, but was angrily attacked by the religious Press, banned by certain libraries and it offended a great many readers, among them Dean Inge and Dame Laurentia. The anonymous author of the tribute to the Abbess entitled *In a Great Tradition,* published after her death, feels that Shaw, badly shaken and distressed by having his wife so near to death, turned to God not with a prayer of thanksgiving at her miraculous escape, but with a stern and critical analysis of the Almighty's actions. Hearing that the book had been written but not yet published, Dame Laurentia wrote to ask Shaw to indicate the line he had adopted. In his reply he said: 'Your letter has given me a terrible fright. The story is absolutely blasphemous, as it goes beyond all the churches and all the gods. I forgot all about you, or I should never have dared. It is about a negro girl converted by a missionary who takes her conversion very seriously and demands where she is to find God. "Seek and ye shall find Him" is the only direction she gets; so off she goes through the forest in her search, with her knobkerrie in her hand. Her search is only too successful. She finds the god of Abraham, and the god of Job; and I regret to say she disposes of both with her knobkerrie. She meets Ecclesiastes (Koheleth) the preacher, who thinks that death reduces life to futility and warns her not to be righteous overmuch. She meets Micah, roaring like a dragon and denouncing the god of Abraham as a bloodthirsty impostor with his horrible sacrifices. She meets Pavlov, who assures her that there is no god, and that life is only a series of reflexes.'

And so he goes on until he smashes the Cross to pieces. There is a repeated profanation of divine names and ideas. He ends his letter strangely: 'As I want you to go on praying for me I must in common honesty let you know what you are praying for. I have a vision of a novice innocently praying for that good man Bernard Shaw, and a scandalised Deity exclaiming "What! That old reprobate who lives in Whitehall Court, for whom purgatory is too good. Don't dare mention him in my presence. . . ." Shall I send you the story or not? It is very irreverent and iconoclastic but I don't think *you* will think it fundamentally irreligious.'

She asked to see the book and was sent a complete set of printer's proofs. To her it was a grotesque parody of the Christian truths she held to be most sacred and she upbraided and censured the author. Shaw had by this time set out on a tour of the world, and her letter reached him in Siam. It was stolen by a Shavian admirer during the voyage, and so was his reply, which never reached her. But he wrote her another letter to say that 'even my callousness was pierced by finding that it (the book) had shocked and distressed you'.

To the end of her life she could hardly bring herself to mention the book. 'The open rejection of our Lord's divinity and the mockery of the Crucifix by one whom she had come to regard as a dear friend filled her with grief and indignation; she felt utterly crushed and humiliated', the anonymous writer of the tribute states. What she feared was that the book might easily gain a mastery over young and impressionable minds. Their friendship was broken off and it was not until September 1934 that Dame Laurentia, on the advice of a friend, sent him a card to mark the Papal blessing on her attaining her Golden Jubilee at Stanbrook. The card, inscribed 'In Memory of Sept 6 1884–1934 Dame Laurentia McLachlan Abbess of Stanbrook', gave Shaw the impression that it was an announcement of her death. His moving letter of condolence to the community at Stanbrook so touched the Abbess that she wrote and asked him to call and see her. But the friendship was never the same again, for she made no secret of her deep displeasure. This was not, however, shared by all at Stanbrook. In an analysis of the dispute the writer of the tribute to Dame Laurentia draws attention to Shaw's insistence that he was 'inspired' to write the book: the claim is made in the first line of the final chapter; and Shaw goes on, 'I hold, as firmly as St Thomas Aquinas, that all truths, ancient or modern, are divinely inspired.' That Shaw was in face deeply religious at heart is evident from the words in the Epilogue – 'Mere agnosticism leads nowhere.' The writer of the tribute draws this final conclusion: 'Many critics, and none more convincingly than G K Chesterton, have dwelt on Bernard Shaw the Puritan. To regard GBS as an "atheist" in the style of popular newspaper reports is, needless to say, sheer nonsense. He could not or would not, however, seek God in anything physical or symbolical. Even Christ Himself comes between God and Shaw, not indeed as He ought, in the sense of a bridge between God and man, the Way, the Truth and the Life, but as an obstacle like some barbed-wire entanglement to be ruthlessly and impatiently removed at all costs.'

9

Mrs Patrick Campbell

OF THE MANY women to whom Shaw poured out his devotion in extravagant phrases, the only one whom he really loved was the beautiful, witty and highly temperamental actress Mrs Patrick Campbell – 'Stella' to her friends. That is evident in his letters to her and has lingered in the memory of those who knew him.

When the correspondence began he was already married to Charlotte. The marriage was at that time, the 12th April 1899, nine months old. Stella was thirty-four and Shaw nine years her senior; he was known then only as a dramatic critic; she was at the height of her fame as an actress. Writing from the house he and his wife had rented at Hindhead, Shaw states: 'We have this house until the 14th May only; so come quickly. Mrs Shaw will be delighted to see you.' Mrs Campbell did not go and as the romance developed Mrs Shaw firmly refused to see her.

Mrs Patrick Campbell had won fame overnight as an actress six years earlier in Sir Arthur Pinero's play *The Second Mrs Tanqueray*, about a woman with a past (it showed the strong influence of Ibsen); and the purpose of Shaw's letter was to ask her to play the leading rôle in *Caesar and Cleopatra*, which he had written for her and Forbes-Robertson a few months earlier. Her reply has been lost, but she never appeared in it, though Forbes-Robertson did when it was performed in New York seven years later.

A very few letters passed between them until 1912 when the correspondence really got going. They were still

'Mr' and 'Mrs' to each other. In these intervening years Mrs Patrick Campbell had scored a number of resounding successes, the most notable being her remarkable performances as Hedda Gabler in Ibsen's play in 1907 and in a dramatisation of Robert Hichins's novel *Bella Donna* in December 1911. Shaw too had been scoring successes. His most recent was with *Fanny's First Play* in 1911. He had written it for Granville-Barker's wife Lillah McCarthy. The play was presented at the Little Theatre in London and ran for six hundred performances – Shaw's first long run.

In the following year, 1912, he wrote *Pygmalion*, the idea for which had been buzzing round his head for fifteen years, for he wrote to Ellen Terry about it in 1897 – even then he had Mrs Patrick Campbell in mind for it. There have been many attempts at trying to trace the source of Shaw's inspiration for this play. One suggestion, made by R F Rattray, is that while he was sitting in Rodin's studio in Paris for his bust by that great French sculptor, he remembered the classical legend of Pygmalion, the statue with which the sculptor had fallen in love; but that was in 1906, nine years after the idea for the play had occurred to him. Sir Barry Jackson, who was responsible some years later for the Malvern Festivals, where so many of Shaw's plays were presented, quotes the German dramatic critics as saying that Shaw actually found the plot in Tobias Smollett's novel *Humphrey Clinker*. 'The plot is so close,' says Jackson, 'that I challenged GBS about it. I said: "You've been reading your Smollett." He replied: "I can't remember doing that." Then he quickly changed the subject, which he was fond of doing when he wanted to avoid being pressed further. I think he must have read *Humphrey Clinker* years ago in the British Museum and it remained tucked away in the back of his brain.'

When at last Shaw had written the play he took it along to Mrs Patrick Campbell and read it to her. Writing to him the next day, she thanks him for 'letting me hear the play, and for thinking I can be your pretty slut. I wonder if I can please you. I want you to tell me what the business proposal is – when, where and with whom. Perhaps you can come and see me. We said so little yesterday. I mustn't lose time – my days are numbered surely. It was a great pleasure to me to see you again – Yours sincerely B S Campbell.' (Her first name was Beatrice.)

Shaw lost no time in going to see her again; he was back in her house within twenty-four hours. We know nothing of what happened at that meeting, what was discussed with regard to business, and by what personal exchange the romance was kindled. He hugged his ecstasy for two or three days and wrote to her on the 30th June on two sides of a postcard: 'Many thanks for Friday and for a Saturday of delightful dreams. I did not believe that I had that left in me.' (He was fifty-six.) 'I am all right now, down on earth again with all my cymbals and side-drums and blaring vulgarities in full blast; but it would be meanly cowardly to pretend that you are not a very wonderful lady, or that the spell did not work most enchantingly on me for fully twelve hours – GBS.' For the resuscitated philanderer the magic had clearly begun to work again.

Three days later a long letter arrived for her, beginning with the word 'Beatricissima' and ending 'at your feet – GBS'. Though it was a business letter for the most part, it was sprinkled with such phrases as 'Oh beautifullest of all the stars' and 'O Stella Stellarum'. Stella's reply was brief. It began: 'I haven't had a minute to answer your many funny green pages – I wish you weren't so early-Victorian!' It ended with 'My love to you and to your Charlotte too – Beatrice Stella.'

Shaw, with his thoughts focussed on *Pygmalion*, wrote again two days later: 'I want my Liza and I want my Higgins. . . . I must have my Liza and no other Liza. There is no other Liza and can be no other Liza. I wrote the play to have my Liza. And I must have a proper

Higgins for my Liza. I won't listen to reason: I will sit there and howl. I can howl for twenty years, getting louder and louder all the time.'

Her reply was affectionate. 'Oh darling what a letter! I call you "darling" because "dear Mr Shaw" means nothing at all – whilst "darling" means "most dear". After this the correspondence became brisk. He poured out his affection in extravagant superlatives and sent her numerous photographs of himself. She wrote at last: 'I do wish you wouldn't send me your photographs – I dislike photographs, I have given all yours away at the theatre – my dresser particularly liked the one of you as Jesus Christ playing the piano.'

This went on for two years – letters from various parts of Europe ('Stella, Stella; all the winds of the north are musical with the thousand letters I have written to you on this journey'). Occasional ditties about 'Stella' and 'Stellinita', and numerous references to cuts, corrections and interpolations in *Pygmalion*. When she was ill, Shaw wrote: 'You must be either better or dead. Say, oh fairest, is your excellent white bosom still straightened, or are you up and about?' She replied: 'Well darling, I am not in heaven. . . and what bosom is left me is still straightened. In a week they say I shall be able to sit up. . . . I send you my love – mind you come Monday or Tuesday – Stella.' And again she wrote: 'Then tomorrow Thursday at four o'clock and you'll bring *Androcles and the Lion*' – which he wrote in 1912 – 'even if I would rather talk than read.' A few days later yet another letter from Stella: 'Oh dear me – it's too late to do anything but *accept* you and *love* you – but when you were quite a little boy somebody ought to have said "hush" just once!' And again: 'If you give me one kiss and you can only kiss me if I say "kiss me" and I will never say "kiss me" because I am a respectable widow and I wouldn't let any man kiss me unless I was sure of a wedding-ring.'

A few weeks later she was no longer coy. Writing on

5th February 1913, she capitulated; her letter ends with twenty-two x's for kisses, followed by the words 'and so on – and so on – and so on – and so on. . . .'

Shaw was ecstatic. Writing the next day he said: 'When I am dead let them put an inscription on 12 Hinde St *Here a great man found happiness.*' He had apparently been to see her, for he adds: 'I was only twenty minutes late for my appointment; and if I had been wise enough to miss it altogether I should have saved £300; for that is what it cost me in money' – he does not tell us how. 'What it cost me in absence three hundred millions could not pay for.' And in the following month, March: 'I MUSTN'T be in love; but I AM. You have beaten me – my first defeat, and my first success.' Does that suggest that he had an *affaire* with her? Some think not; others think that this may have been the only instance when intimacy took place. He had photographed her lying in bed and there is a significant, though a little obscure, allusion to it in a letter he sent her from Dublin in April 1913: 'When you said you were writing in bed, I asked myself was it a wild hope or a wild fear? Oh the Life Force never laid a deeper trap than that illness that gained for me the entry to the sanctuary. I should know what to do now that you are up.'

A month later, on the 24th May 1913, Shaw had a most distressing shock: his conversation with Stella on the telephone from his (initially Charlotte's) London home was overheard by his wife. He describes it in a letter to Stella. 'I am all torn to bits: you don't know what it is to me to be forced to act artificially when everything has just been freshly stirred in me. It gives me a sort of *angina pectoris*; all the fibres round my chest begin to sing and stir and drag and pull in a way that would make anyone else wild, and makes me set my face grimly.

'But the worst of it is that all our conversation was overheard; and the effect was dreadful; it hurts me miserably to see anyone suffer like that. I must, it seems, murder myself or else murder her. It will pass over;

106

but in the meantime here is a lovely spring day murdered.

'Well, I dare say it is good for us all to suffer; but it is hard that the weak should suffer most. If I could be human and suffer with a suffering of my own, there would be some poetic justice in it; but I can't: I can only feel the sufferings of others with a pain that pity makes, and with a fierce impatience of the unreasonableness of it – the essential inhumanity of this jealousy that I never seem to escape from' – a revelation that Charlotte was constantly jealous and doubtless was given cause to be so. 'And it is a comfort at least,' he adds, 'that you also have the unquenchable gaiety of genius, and can stand anything. This much breaks out of me; I must say it. Now I can go back doggedly to work and write tragedies. And believe that you cannot possibly have wanted a run through the lanes with me on this summer day more than I. I throw my desperate hands to heaven and ask why one cannot make one beloved woman happy without sacrificing another. We are all slaves of what is best within us and worst without us – GBS.'

No comment appears to have been made by Stella about this until ten days later, when all she said then was: 'Poor you. It's quite stupid nothing can be done to prevent your suffering.' Then she talked about other things; she was going to a supper-party (not a 'bohemian merry-making') that was being given by Lady Wemyss, where George Cornwallis-West was to be present. He was a gay man about town, well connected – his sister was married to the Prince of Pless and he himself had married Lady Randolph Churchill, Winston Churchill's mother, but that marriage was breaking up, and he was to marry Mrs Patrick Campbell a few months later – he was nine years her junior. Shaw, aware of this possibility, wrote: 'He is young and I am old; so let him wait until I am tired of you. This cannot in the course of nature be long. . . . About you I am a mass of illusions. It is impossible that I should not tire soon; nothing so wonderful could last. You cannot really be what you are to me; you are a figure from the dreams of my boyhood – all romance. . . . I promise to tire as soon as I can so as to leave you free. I will produce *Pygmalion* and criticise your acting. I will yawn over your adorable silly sayings and ask myself are they really amusing. I will run after other women in search of a new attachment; I will hurry through my dream as fast as I can; only let me have my dream out.'

She didn't. In less than two months, trouble blew up between them. In his numerous letters during that interval he almost suffocated her with his loving endearments – 'Ever blessedest darling. . . . Dearest Sillybilly. . . . Oh treasurest. . . . Oh loveliest'; and sometimes she too was exceedingly affectionate, but she had her moments of almost brutal irritation. On the 9th July Shaw wrote: 'Stella: don't play with me. You know very well you have only to look noble and hurt, the least tiniest shade in the world, and my heart of stone turns to water; and this you mustn't do merely for fun – cat-and-mouse – not in the least that I grudge you the fun, but because you wouldn't know what to do with me when I came back, and would have to be horrid to get rid of me again. When you shut the door on me the other day with a forced smile, and said "Ouf!" when it slammed, I said, "So it has lasted only a month after all!" And then I remembered that it began in the middle of the summer, and lasted a whole year. I have been a saint for your sake for a whole year. . . . And not until the year was out did you say "Go and love somebody else and don't bother me. . . ." Stella: you mustn't deride: you must remember that other people have souls as well as you, and that if they hold them up before God with the scars of wounds inflicted by you, He will not even throw you into hell: He will stamp you out with His foot.'

Early in August she had decided to go to the sea where she wanted to be alone, she said. Shaw went to see her in her house in London on the 6th and she wrote to him the next day: 'You were all kindness and sympathy yesterday. . . . When you are tender a thousand cherubs peep out of your purple and black wings – It's getting difficult not to love you more than I ought to love you – Offend me again quickly to pull me together – But by the sea I must be alone – You know. Stella.' Only the day before, when he had come to see her, he had written: 'When I am solitary you are always with me. When you are solitary by the sea, where shall I be? Where, Stella? Where, where, where?' But she was insistent that he should not join her. Had George Cornwallis-West planned to be with her? Shaw nevertheless ignored her pleas and followed her there. On learning that he had arrived and was staying at the same hotel, The Guildford in Sandwich, she sent a note to his room, dated 10th August 1913. 'Please will you go back to London today – or go where-ever you like but don't stay here – If you won't go I must – I am very tired and I oughtn't to go another journey. Please don't make me despise you.'

Shaw replied on a coloured postcard, headed 'The Guildford Hotel, Sandwich', but posted at Ramsgate. It said briefly: 'The Desolate Shore' – possibly a pun on 'Shaw' – and 'The Lights of Ramsgate'. She replied at once: 'Goodbye. I am still tired – you were more fit for a journey than I.' And she left at once.

This made him very angry. 'Very well, go,' he wrote, 'the loss of a woman is not the end of the world. The sun shines: it is pleasant to swim: it is good to work: my soul can stand alone. But I am deeply, deeply, deeply wounded. . . . Bah! You have no nerve: you have no brain: you are the caricature of an eighteenth-century male sentimentalist, a Hedda Gabler titivated with odds and ends from Burne-Jones's ragbag: you know nothing, God help you, except what you know all wrong. . . . You have wounded my vanity – an inconceivable audacity, an unpardonable crime. Farewell, wretch that I loved.'

That wasn't, however, the end of it. He wrote again that evening: 'Oh, my rancour is not slaked: I have not said enough vile things to you. What are you, miserable

wretch, that my entrails should be torn asunder hour
after hour? Of that fifty-seven years I have suffered
twenty and worked thirty-seven. Then I had a moment's
happiness. . . . I risked the breaking of deep roots and
sanctified ties.'

Two days later she sent him a placatory note: 'You
vagabond you – you blind man. You weaver of words,
you – black and purple winged hider of cherubs – you
poor thing unable to understand a mere woman. My
friend all the same. No daughters to relieve your cravings
– no babes to stop your satirical chatterings. Why should
I pay for all your shortcomings. . . . My friend, my dear
friend all the same. Stella.'

Soon all was well again. The letters went on. On the
5th January 1914 she wrote: 'Such a wonderful beautiful
letter. . . . If I could write letters like you, I would write
letters to God.' The plans for *Pygmalion* went on too.
She was to play Eliza Doolittle, and Shaw was to take
her through the rehearsals. Just before these started in
the following month, Stella wrote: 'Oh goodness we're in
for it – and let's be *very* clever – he's fixed' – that meant
that Sir Herbert Tree was to play Higgins – 'and you
can manage the lot of us – and then indeed you'll be a
great man! He wants to be friendly and his admiration
for you and the play is ENORMOUS. I'll be tame as a
mouse and oh so obedient.' She wasn't, nor was Tree,
nor was Shaw for that matter. By April she was writing:
'You haven't hurt me at all. You have only bored me by
your ceaseless teasing and braggarting. I wanted you to
produce the play, and Tree not to be sufficiently insulted
by you as to "throw it up" – in this I have succeeded –
though there are a few more days!!! For myself the last
three months and more particularly the last five days,
have been full of anxiety.'

The greatest anxiety was caused by Stella herself
just before the opening night of *Pygmalion* at His
Majesty's Theatre in London. They had been rehearsing
hard for weeks and found themselves in the most appal-

ling dilemma when, without any warning at all, she failed to turn up for the rehearsal on the morning of the 6th April; she had gone off to marry George Cornwallis-West at the register office in Kensington, and then went away for a brief honeymoon to Crowborough in Sussex. On that very morning the bridegroom's divorce decree from Lady Randolph Churchill had been made absolute. The bride returned, however, a day or two later and sent Shaw a good wishes letter: 'All success to you tonight. It's nice to think of your friendship and your genius – I'll obey orders faithfully. I am so thankful you carried through your giant's work to the finish.' The audience loved the play, but Stella felt that the first use of that word 'bloody' on the stage almost ruined it: 'People laughed too much,' she said.

The long run *Pygmalion* should have had was interrupted by Tree after three months. This had nothing to do with the fact that the First World War appeared to be looming on the horizon and did in fact break out five weeks later. It was withdrawn because Tree said he was tired, though it was generally thought that he was hurt by Shaw's lack of appreciation of his performance as Professor Higgins. Shaw's criticisms had been severe, and Tree said, of his long letters of advice and comment: 'I will not go so far as to say that all people who write letters of more than eight pages are mad, but it is a curious fact that all madmen write letters of more than eight pages.' Shaw was equally sharp with Stella: 'Good God!' he told her, 'you are forty years too old for Eliza; sit still and it is not so noticeable.'

Tree went to Marienbad in Germany for a holiday, having already made £13,000 from that short run of the play. Stella Patrick Campbell took *Pygmalion* to America in October and after a run in New York, toured with it in the United States all through 1915. Her marriage to George Cornwallis-West did not last long. He deserted her in 1919 and waited until her death to marry for the third time.

Stella died in 1940 at the age of seventy-five. Her last years were sad. She had done little work in the theatre. The great actress was shunned by managers because she was temperamental, often very rude, and had for some time been unable to remember her lines. As early as December 1921 she started worrying Shaw about letting her publish his letters to her. He refused point-blank: 'You say you will behave like a perfect gentleman,' he wrote. 'Well a gentleman does not kiss and tell; so that settles *that*.' The copyright was his and there must be no publication while Charlotte was alive. But she went on and on. 'God defend me from idiots,' he wrote; but she was not to be deterred. In 1928 her pleas became far more urgent. Shaw, refusing to budge, suggested a benefit performance at some theatre to raise money for her. 'I wonder could we get you a Civil List Pension. How many Cabinet Ministers have you insulted?'

Stella wrote again: 'I am told that in America your letters to me are worth £200 each – those of eight and ten pages – more – I have 93 – £20,000. Also I am told the only way I can prevent their being published there (I would like them published they are so lovely – one in particular should be placed between two leaves of gold) – is to have 12 copies published here – Now please don't be too busy to remember that I love you, and you love me and come any time tomorrow Friday between 3 pm and 2 am. My love to you, Stella.'

But he would not agree. 'Selling letters has nothing to do with their publication,' he wrote. 'The letters are worth a good deal. . . . There are two ways of selling: (1) by private contract to some dealer; (2) by sending the letters to Sotheby's to be sold by auction. In the latter case the auctioneer is apt to quote appetising passages in the catalogue. They are picked up and broadcast by the Press' – and that, of course, Shaw did not want done during Charlotte's lifetime. He summed it up with an air of finality in the following verse:

When I am dead, my dearest,
Sing no sad songs for me
But cast my spells on Mister Wells
And ask a handsome fee.

The reference is to Mr Gabriel Wells, the American dealer in manuscripts and letters. Stella sold him Shaw's *Widowers' Houses* (possibly the manuscript of the play or an autographed copy of it in book form) for £100; and on informing Shaw of this, she added: 'So you see you are still helping me financially.'

At that time Shaw was writing *The Apple Cart*. In it he portrayed Stella as Orinthia, King Magnus's beautiful 'diversion', who urges him to divorce his wife and marry her, but he will not hear of it. The scene ends with the two struggling with each other and rolling about the floor. Stella had heard of this and was greatly distressed. She wrote at once to Shaw 'DD writes, "G B Shaw has just put you into his play as the Egira of the King. This lady is supported by the Civil List – with rooms in Buckingham Palace – and that you want to be Queen." ' Stella was aware that many would recognise Orinthia as a portrayal of herself. She had always been extremely eager to meet Shaw's wife and had often referred to her in her letters, and doubtless also in her talks with him. But Charlotte had always refused very firmly to meet her. Once Stella suggested that they should make up a party and go to the theatre together, but Mrs Shaw said NO. Shaw tried to explain this by saying that when he told Charlotte that 'Stella cannot understand why you don't love her', Charlotte had replied: 'That shows some good in her.' Even Stella's invitation to a supper-party after the first night of the revival of *The Second Mrs Tanqueray* was declined: 'The company would have been fit for your lady,' Stella wrote ruefully afterwards.

Now, writing to Stella from Dubrovnik to describe the Orinthia scene in his new play, Shaw said: 'That the scene is amusingly scandalous and even disgraceful (though **Platonic**) is undeniable. One or two passages will not be new to you.... I don't believe you could (or would) play it; but you would most certainly play the devil with the whole production, and perhaps make me behave badly and leave me ten years older, which is more than I can afford at seventy-two.'

Stella conveyed to him her grave anxiety that so many people already knew that Orinthia was really Stella herself. 'How can it be a "secret" between us', she wrote, 'when Edith Evans told me that she was playing *me*. It is unkind of you not to keep your promise to read this play, or send it to me.'

Shaw's answer was far from reassuring: 'Edith Evans guessed, of course,' he wrote. 'DD (the Hon Mrs Alfred Lyttelton) knows; B – knows; Nancy (Lady Astor) knows; perhaps half a dozen others know (or think they know: for only you and I will ever know); but the Press must never get hold of it.'

Again Stella protested: 'I haven't felt at all inclined to answer this last letter and I don't know why I do – You should have sent me your play to read. You are out of tune with friendship and simple courtesy.'

Finally he took the play and read the scene out to her. She was greatly upset. Rehearsals had already begun. On returning home Shaw made some modest revisions. 'Do you mind if it runs this way?' he asked.

"*Orinthia:* I can give you beautiful, wonderful children; have you ever seen a lovelier boy than my Basil?

Magnus: Your children are beautiful; but they are fairy children; and I have several very real ones already. A divorce would sweep them out of the way of fairies. . . ."

'And so to make it *our* immortal play I have changed –

"*Orinthia:* It is out of the question; your dream of being queen must remain a dream"

to

"*Orinthia:* We are only two children at play; and you must be content to be my queen in fairyland."

114

'Does that cure the soreness at your heart? It makes mine feel much better.'

But Stella was not satisfied. The whole thing seemed to her to be 'dreadfully commonplace and vulgar'; and she added, 'Why make Orinthia run down your wife? That isn't funny from any point of view – but the kitchen's. Has Charlotte ever heard that I asked you to show her your letters to me, and that I didn't know until after I had sent them back to Hutchinson – blackened out in spots by you – that you hadn't done so – a letter I had of yours mentions this. . . . As you sat in my room yesterday and read to me – I suddenly knew you – saw you.'

Shaw replied: 'The world may very well laugh at us; but it had better have splendid fun than dirty fun. . . . Perhaps I should not have come; but how else could you have heard the scene?'

Stella talked of lawyers. She wrote: 'If I had the script here I would talk it over with my lawyer – I am sure in its suggestiveness it is libellous and ought not to be presented. Tear it up, and re-write it with every scrap of the mischievous vulgarism omitted, and all suburban backchat against Charlotte and suggested harlotry against me, and the influence of your own superiority wiped out.' He answered flatly: 'Dearest – you are a fool! Oh, such a, *such* a, *SUCH* a fool! Goodnight – GBS.' And so the scene remained.

The letters were not published even after Charlotte's death in 1943; they had to wait until after Shaw's death in 1950. He had agreed to their being published then in order that Stella's great-grandchildren should benefit from the royalties.

Mrs Patrick Campbell's advancing age and inability to find work brought many financial anxieties. She wrote to Shaw on 1st February 1939 shortly after *Pygmalion* had been filmed by Gabriel Pascal: 'I heard again what a tremendous success *Pygmalion* is and that it comes to London in June – that Pascal has to account to you for

10% of the total receipts – you can't have *invested* that money yet! Christmas-box time has passed – and the New Year – but my birthday is on the 9th of this month.'

Her last letter to him was written from her solitary room in a Paris pension on the 28th June 1939, a few months before her death. 'I am getting used to poverty and discomfort, and even to the very real unhappiness of having no maid to take a few of the little daily cares from me, and give me an arm when I cross the road carrying "Moonbeam" through the terrifying roaring traffic.'

Shortly after this, unexpectedly, a note arrived from Bernard Shaw. Stella was so affected by it that, with tears coursing down her cheeks, she held it out with a trembling hand for a friend to see. It was a cheque from Shaw for £4,000.

The friend, haunted even now by this touching memory, said: 'It was a personal, private moment and I don't want to be linked with it at all. I mention it only because GBS did respond in the end to Stella's appeal and was not as hard-hearted and callous as so many people seem to think.'

10
His Greatest Years

DURING THE YEARS that Mrs Patrick Campbell's fame was on the decline, Shaw's kept rising until the world came to recognise and accept him as a great playwright and a dazzling wit. It was not a meteoric rise. The First World War came on the heels of the rousing success of *Pygmalion* but the public hostility to his anti-war writings and speeches rose to fever pitch and lingered for years after the war had ended. Meanwhile he went on writing plays. Many of them were just playlets. It was with *Heartbreak House,* which took him six years (1913–1919), that he broke through to world prominence. It was his thirty-sixth play and was first seen in New York in November 1920, with a London performance a year later. Set in a leisured, cultured Europe in the pre-war years and strongly influenced by Tchekhov's *Cherry Orchard* and *The Seagull*, it was regarded by Shaw as 'One of the best things I have ever done'. It was not, however, an immediate success; in London it was a failure; after a month's run it was unable to average more than £39 a performance. Shaw was greatly distressed, but the skill of the characterisation and the richness of its dialogue led to it being eventually recognised as one of Shaw's finest plays.

He had in the meantime completed a cycle of five new plays, which bear the overall title of *Back to Methuselah*. Called a play about Creative Evolution, it is a vast extension, into the past and the future, of his unshakable belief that woman is the hunter, seeking the male solely for the purpose of perpetuating the species, to achieve which she uses all her seductive wiles. He had used this theme in *Man and Superman*, which he wrote nearly twenty years earlier, with the Superman seeking something better than just enslavement by sex for the fulfilment of woman's desires. *Back to Methuselah* starts in the Garden of Eden with Adam and Eve, the Serpent, and Cain and Abel, then jumps forward nearly 6,000 years to AD 1920, and moves by shorter stages to AD 2170, then to AD 3000 and finally to the year AD 31,920, called 'As Far as Thought Can Reach'. Into this cycle he poured much of his philosophy and his religious beliefs, which echoed and elaborated thoughts he had expressed before. In 1922, two years after the five plays were written, they had their first production in New York, and towards the end of the following year Barry Jackson put them on singly, and later in a single marathon session at the Royal Court Theatre in London. With it Shaw attracted world attention, but did not yet attain his greatest triumph. That came with *Joan*, which he wrote in 1923; it was performed at the New Theatre in London with Sybil Thorndike as Joan on the 26th March 1924, following a New York presentation in the preceding December.

Sybil Thorndike first met Shaw in 1908: Lewis Casson, whom she married that year, had got to know him while understudying Granville-Barker in *Candida*. Sybil, just back from a theatrical tour of America, had been invited to understudy the part of Miss Proserpine Garrett in *Candida*. But at the rehearsal 'Shaw roared with laughter', Sybil told me. 'He said, "Splendid, my dear young lady. Now go home and have children – then you can play the title rôle of *Candida*." I played it quite a lot later on, but I wasn't accepted by Shaw then.

'It was in 1919 while rehearsing *Candida* and appearing in *The Trojan Women* and *Medea* in a season of matinées at the Holborn Empire, that I got to know Shaw. At the time he was also rehearsing Stella Patrick Campbell for a revival of *Pygmalion* and used to come to us absolutely whacked. But he took our rehearsals with extraordinary vigour and was most exacting. Always polite, he never made any of us feel uncomfortable; but if actor or actress put on airs GBS never failed to admonish them with a snub.

'One evening, after attending a performance of, I think it was, *The Trojan Women*, GBS while walking down Holborn said to his wife: "I am going home to write *St Joan*." This surprised Charlotte. She had been urging him for years to write a play about Joan of Arc and had assembled all the historical facts for him, but he had always refused. She asked him now what made him change his mind. He replied: "I have found at last someone who can play St Joan." He meant me.

'I was, of course, thrilled and extremely flattered when I learned that he was writing the play for me. It is a great play and there is a tremendous depth of religious feeling in it. GBS arranged a special performance of *Joan* for the nuns and priests of St Theresa. They formed the entire audience in the theatre, and I remember the laughter of these very holy Carmelite nuns – I can hear it now – they actually rocked with laughter during the amusing scenes in *St Joan*; the comedy was there, and there was no reason why those who had taken the vow shouldn't laugh.'

Miles Malleson, the character actor and playwright, said, 'Shaw informed me that he had written the part of the Dauphin especially for me. I was looking forward to it, but heard nothing more until Sybil Thorndike and Lewis Casson told me one day that during the casting Shaw had announced that he did not want me to play the Dauphin; they added that they were greatly distressed at the change. Not long afterwards I was walking along Adelphi Terrace and, as I was entering the Savage Club, Shaw hailed me. "Miles," he said, "you know I wrote the part of the Dauphin for you, but the Cassons don't want you to play it." I was puzzled. Surely Sybil and Lewis wouldn't have fabricated what they had said to me. They were not that sort of people. I'm afraid Shaw must have changed his mind and, in order to soften the blow, put the blame on them. In the end Ernest Thesiger played the Dauphin and he did it very well.

'I wouldn't want anyone to think that I have any sort of grudge against GBS. He did me a great kindness some years before and I have never forgotten it. After being invalided out of the Army during the First World War, I wrote a play called *The Fanatics*. I had seen German prisoners and wounded soldiers of both sides, with their arms and legs missing, and I felt, "This is a bloody silly business!" When I returned home the war was still on. I went to an anti-war meeting at which Bertrand Russell was the principal speaker – he was arrested after the meeting and sent to prison. My play was anti-war, and no theatre manager would look at it. Shaw, who had a financial interest in the *New Statesman*, produced a fairly large supplement entitled "The Truth about the War", in which he said things that nobody would disagree with today. But such views were unpopular then and Shaw didn't like being unpopular. Seeing me walking along the street shortly afterwards he crossed the road to talk to me, and spoke with great feeling of his unpopularity. "I think I am finished!" he said. Then he went on to say that he was writing a play about St Joan and asked me to go with him to his flat for a talk. He described his play, walking up and down the room with long strides, then suddenly stopped at the bust of himself by Rodin. "What do you think of it?" he asked me. I said, "It's a magnificent piece of work." But Shaw disagreed. "It's a horrible thing," he said, "horrible, because it gets younger every day." It was during the course of our talk that I mentioned my play *The Fanatics* and told him of the managers' strong opposition to it. "Let me see it," he said. "I think I might be able to do something with it." I sent him the manuscript and he showed it to Victor Gollancz, who was at that time with the publisher Ernest Benn. He published the play in book form, which helped to get it known, and eventually it was produced. So I had much to be grateful to Shaw for.'

Miles Malleson had known Shaw well for some years and had appeared in Shaw's *Fanny's First Play* as far back as 1911. 'At one of the rehearsals Dorothy Minto, who was playing the part of Darling Dora, was late in arriving because she had missed her bus and Shaw said he would read her part. He did it well, but in the middle of the reading he suddenly threw the book into the air and exclaimed: "By God, this is a brilliant play!"

'I found it really quite remarkable that Shaw, who had never acted on the stage himself, actually knew all the actor's problems by instinct. I had quite a long speech to deliver in that play as Trotter, *The Times* critic. Shaw came up to me during the rehearsal and pointed to the passage. He said: "During this speech the audience will begin to shuffle and cough by the time you've got halfway through it. You will no doubt then try to rush through the rest of it. You mustn't do that. You must *slow down* your pace, not rush it. Say it at a very slow speed." By God, he was right. The audience found that they had to listen as my speed slowed down, and there was no coughing or shuffling.

'When Shaw was on the Board of Governors of the Royal Academy of Dramatic Art, he asked me to lunch and pumped me about the faults and the good points in the organisation. He took immense interest in everything he undertook and went conscientiously into every detail of their numerous activities.

'He was also very clever to keep his more outrageous personal opinions out of his plays. Instead he put them into his prefaces, which were published when the plays were issued in book form; he realised that the people seated in the stalls would never bother to read his prefaces. What they came to see were his plays and in them it was the characters who aired their own fantastic views, and Shaw never lost the opportunity of describing these characters in the plays as "mad". The public laughed

121

at the characters and it was from the plays that Shaw eventually made his money.'

A gap of six years separated *St Joan* from Shaw's next play *The Apple Cart*. He had been inactive as a dramatist during that interval and wrote *The Apple Cart* especially for the Malvern Festival where it was given its first English production by Barry Jackson in August 1929 and was brought to London four weeks later. Cedric Hardwicke played King Magnus and Edith Evans was Orinthia. All who knew of Shaw's romantic relationship with Mrs Patrick Campbell could not fail to identify them in these two characters; even Stella's attempts to detain him, sometimes by force, after the *Pygmalion* rehearsals in order to keep him from hurrying home to Charlotte, had been worked into the play where we see Orinthia exercising similar wiles to keep King Magnus from returning to his wife.

Cedric Hardwicke told me: 'It is to my association with Shaw that I owe my emergence as an actor of any real stature.' He had appeared in some of Shaw's earlier plays – *Heartbreak House*, the cycle of *Back to Methuselah* and *Caesar and Cleopatra*. During the rehearsal of the last, Shaw told him: 'I call this play *Caesar and Cleopatra* not *Caesar versus Cleopatra*. Cleopatra is not a difficult part, Caesar is – Caesar is worth half a dozen Hamlets.'

Barry Jackson, having selected the attractive town of Malvern in the Worcestershire hills as the setting for the Shaw Festival, induced the Town Council to rebuild their playhouse for the purpose and thus provide a home for Shaw's plays such as Shakespeare had at Stratford-on-Avon.

'We started our rehearsals at the Old Vic in London,' Cedric Hardwicke added. 'Shaw, tall and lean, strode on to the bare stage, looking half like God and half like a very malicious satyr. He sat down at a table in the centre of the stage and began to read the play in his soft Irish voice, every syllable clearly enunciated. That was what he demanded from his actors and we got the full force of his wrath and scorn if our pronunciation ever fell short of that standard. "You make 'Life Force' sound like 'live horse' ", he would say. He went further than just that. He used the inflexions of his voice to differentiate each character. It was an astonishing performance. We were tremendously impressed by his mental and physical stamina. He was at that time only a few days from his seventy-third birthday. Shaw always insisted that the audience was required to use its brain. The theatre is "as important as the Church in the Middle Ages. The apostolic succession," he said, "from Aeschylus to myself is as serious and as continuously inspired as that younger institution, the apostolic succession of the Christian Church." '

Among the Shaw plays put on by Barry Jackson at Malvern were *Pygmalion* and *St Joan*, in both of which Wendy Hiller played the lead. Though she was then only twenty-two, Shaw, who had seen her in *Love on the Dole*, selected her himself for these rôles.

'Barry Jackson paid me £20 a week,' Wendy told me, 'and Ernest Thesiger possibly got the same sum for playing Professor Higgins in *Pygmalion*; he wore a small beard for the part, and a knickerbocker suit just like Shaw's. We had only six rehearsals for each of the two plays. Shaw said this would be enough, they had no time to give us any more. I wasn't fitted for the armour I had to wear in *St Joan*. It was loose and very heavy and when Shaw came up to talk to me about the part, I felt so shy, that I nearly fell backwards. But fortunately I was able to save myself. If I had fallen I would never have been able to get up again.

'I never overcame my shyness during those Malvern years. Shaw was for me, a young actress, the dominating figure in the world of the theatre. He towered above everybody else. During that wonderful summer, when the sun seemed to shine every day, I saw him out walking across the hills every afternoon at four o'clock, while I was on my way to the theatre. He used to wave his stick in a friendly greeting – it was like seeing a legendary figure – Machiavelli or Shakespeare. And he would stop and ask where I was going and when I told him, he would say "So early?" and then add: "You can't keep away from the theatre."

'He asked me once to go with him to see one of the plays in which I was not appearing. We sat together in the front row of the dress circle. His wife Charlotte, who was hard of hearing, sat in one of the boxes. Shaw was in great form – lively, gay; but as soon as the play ended, he turned to me and said with a twinkle: "I cannot see you home, Wendy – I have to go to my wife now." '

Shortly before the outbreak of the Second World War Constance Cummings went to see Shaw to ask if she could play St Joan. 'I don't say I shall be as good as Sybil Thorndike,' she said, 'but I shall be better than some of the others who have played the part, for I at least understand it.

'GBS at this point,' Constance told me with laughter, 'threw up his hands and said: "What impertinence!" Then, after a pause, he added: "Elizabeth Bergner came on to the stage at her very first appearance looking as though she had already been half burned. You can go ahead, my dear, and play St Joan." I did, and he seemed pleased with my performance.'

Three years earlier when Wendy Hiller played St Joan at Malvern, Shaw sent her this analysis of her interpretation of the rôle:

'My dear Wendy – I had another look at *St Joan* and saw you trying your pet stunts for all they were worth. They failed completely, as I told you they would; but I saw what you were driving at, and can now explain to you why they failed. What you have conceived is a cataleptic Joan, who in her highest moments goes up out of the world into a trance. Such an effect is not impossible on the stage if the author has prepared it properly. If the play began with Joan in the fields with her sheep, hearing the bells, and going into a trance of ecstasy ending in a sleep from which she would be awakened by village folk who would discuss this strange power of hers, so that the audience would learn about the trances and be able to recognise their symptoms, then you might produce an electric effect by making such a trance the climax of the Cathedral scene and of the Trial scene too, to say nothing of the epilogue.

'Without such careful preparation the effect is quite impossible. To the unprepared audience the trance appears a collapse, unaccountable and disappointing. When you collapsed at the last moment of the Cathedral scene, with victory just within your grasp, the man next to me threw up his hands in despair and exclaimed "Good God!" To those who remembered Sybil Thorndike's exit it was worse than disappointing: it was infuriating. In the last speech of the Trial, where you have in a few sweeping words to paint a landscape of a frosty morning in the country in the lambing season, and you suddenly try a cataleptic convulsion in which not one word is audible or intelligible, you are simply puzzling. In both cases the result is a complete and astonishing knock-out.

'However, it is a bit of experience for you. One gets experience by making mistakes. In future, when you want to put something into your part that is not in the play, you must ask the author – or some other author – to lead up to the interpolation for you. Never forget that the effect of a line may depend, not on its delivery, but on something said earlier in the play either by somebody else or by yourself, and that if you change it it may be necessary to change the whole first act as well. Now I can't rewrite *Joan* for you, though it would be great fun. I must be faithful to her as well as nice to you; and Joan wasn't a cataleptic. She was forcible and sure from beginning to end, and never played pianissimo – you get pianissimo, which, dearest, you have not yet got the art of making perfectly audible. So deny it to yourself if you can in this play. When you come on in the Trial scene, kick the chain from step to step instead of drag-

125

ging it. Let the kicks be heard before you come on; and when they take it off do not rub your ankle pathetically, but bend your legs at the knees and stretch them as if you were going to take on the whole Court at all-in wrestling. And call the man a noodle heartily, not peevishly. Get a big laugh with it.

'And now go your way in the strength of the Lord; but do not wholly despise the instruction of the old bird – GBS.'

11
Gradual Conversion to Films

THOUGH AN ARDENT film-goer since the earliest short flickering Charlie Chaplin comedies, Shaw was most violently opposed to the presentation of his plays on the screen. This is understandable when one realises that in the days of silent moving pictures it would have involved the sacrifice of almost his entire dialogue, which could only be presented in one-line fragments as captions, and the loss of the long, intricate arguments on which he relied to appeal to the audience and to force it to think. But when talkies came, in 1928, his attitude altered. He saw at once the tremendous opportunity they offered; and a year or so later he went off to Elstree, where British International Pictures had made the first English talkie, to discuss the filming of his *How He Lied to Her Husband*. It was a short play, which he had written in 1904 and its star was to be Edmund Gwenn, who had appeared on the stage in *Captain Brassbound's Conversion* and in the first production of *Man and Superman*. Shaw's secretary, Blanche Patch, who was at Elstree for the rehearsal, says: 'Shaw asked Gwenn to put more life into the fight between the lover and the husband. "I'll show you," he cried to Gwenn. "Come on!" Gwenn did, and in a moment he put Shaw, who was then seventy-four, flat on his back. "You see," said Shaw, getting on to his feet again, "it's quite easy." '

Seeing the play on the screen, Shaw was ecstatic and talked of it with tremendous pride during the Malvern Festival. The following year he embarked on the filming of *Arms and the Man* and could not contain himself on discovering that, instead of talking about the battle in a bedroom, one was able to see the actual battle on the screen. 'The characters can go everywhere,' he exclaimed, 'upstairs and downstairs, into gardens and across mountain country with an ease and freedom that is impossible in a room with three walls, which is all you see on the stage.' If talkies had been invented earlier, he would certainly have been writing cinema scripts as well as plays.

By the time Gabriel Pascal, the Hungarian producer, rang his front-door bell at Whitehall Court a few years later, Shaw was sufficiently receptive to discuss the conversion of his plays into films, for he realised that this new medium would provide him with an audience numbering millions instead of merely thousands. It was an immense target at which to direct his message. But one vital requisite was essential: there must be no alteration of his text. Pascal yielded and a start was made with *Pygmalion* on a scale that far surpassed anything attempted in Shaw's first two screen efforts. An impressive cast was assembled. Leslie Howard was to play Professor Higgins, a choice which did not meet with Shaw's approval, and Wendy Hiller, with whose acting talent Shaw had been greatly impressed at Malvern, was chosen by Shaw himself for the rôle of Eliza Doolittle. Anthony Asquith, a sensitive, artistic, young director, was engaged to direct the film. But over-all control was exercised by Shaw through Pascal at every stage of the film's making.

He bombarded Pascal with letters. Writing on the 24th February 1938 and addressing him as 'Gabriel' instead of 'Gaby', Shaw announced that after giving serious thought to the filming of *Pygmalion*, he knew exactly how to handle the final scenes. Asquith, he said, was talented and inventive, but he was quite wrong to take the audience in the closing scene back to Covent Garden with its 'dirty mob' and to bring Eliza's father, Doolittle, on again, after he had been finished and done with in the story. Nor did he want Higgins and Eliza to be taken out of the lovely drawing room and put into a car just to be shaken up. It was childish and would spoil the effect completely. So away with all that silly stuff!

Careful instructions were also set out for the art director – Shaw overlooked nothing. The art director was Laurence Irving, grandson of Sir Henry Irving, the actor whom Shaw had attacked so ferociously. As the end of the film will depend on Irving, he would have to make the drawing room pretty, with the river visible, if possible, through the windows and the sun shining – 'a perfect day' in fact. The final scene on the embankment at Cheyne Walk must be spacious and really beautiful. Irving must try to eclipse Whistler.

Shaw was sorry he had to put in the flower-shop scene. But there was no need for it to cost much since it was not in Bond Street but in South Kensington. It should be half florist, half greengrocer and fruiterer; and Freddy could be seen weighing property grapes for a lady customer. Old bits of wood could be used for the counters and everything unsightly could be covered up with flowers.

This is an all-British film, he added – no American script writer, but every word written by the author.

The flower-shop scene was one of the new sequences Shaw had been persuaded to write for the film version but it was not used. His continuing interest in the casting and the clothes the leading characters should wear is evident in his next letter.

Shaw insisted that the parts of the supporting players must not be 'over-cast'. Cecil Trouncer would just have to play the big policeman in the scene against the railings – that is all: he must not appear in any of the other scenes. To put him into the scene in which Eliza uses the words 'not bloody likely' would be disastrous.

Told that Jean Cadell would like to appear as the parlourmaid if he could make it a part for her, he refused:

she had been offered one of the best parts in the film and would have been starred if she had accepted it. For her to play the parlourmaid would be most damaging to her professionally.

Violet Vanbrugh, he suggested, would be ideal as the ambassadress in the new ballroom scene: though small, it was a fine part and a most dignified role. And, the idea coming quite suddenly to him, he asked for a black Princess to be introduced into that scene – a negress talking Hottentot – all clicks, with Higgins following her about and taking down the clicks in his notebook. But she would have to be a beautiful and dignified negress.

He mentioned how much the actors and actresses should be paid – fifteen guineas for one, two guineas for another – rather arbitrary, but he gave it just as his estimate; he indicated also which players should not be coached in their parts – it would be a waste of time, he said, as he had used them before in other plays of his and had found them very good: one could not find anyone better, so leave them alone.

Then he explained how the players' names should be listed in the credits – the Rector, O B Clarence; P C Rogerson, Cecil Trouncer; Chelsea Rose, Eileen Beldon; and so on.

All this, he said, had taken up so much of his time that he hadn't been able to think of a way of getting rid of Piccadilly Circus.

Though always ready to agree with Shaw, Pascal sometimes found these precise, pernickety orders very irritating – 'it is a kind of sadism', he said. But then Pascal too was capable of being very pernickety, as, we shall see, when it came to filming *Caesar and Cleopatra*.

But to return to *Pygmalion*. Pascal persisted in wanting just the one policeman, but Shaw was adamant: there *must* be two policemen, he insisted – one aged forty, the other aged twenty; and there would have to be two scenes to give the impression that the two young lovers have had to run as far as Cavendish Square from the first policeman, and as far as Hanover Square from the second policeman. And furthermore, he went on, Trouncer must speak only *one* line, not two.

He was incensed at the suggestion that his script would have to be passed by the American Motion Picture Producers Association – 'amateur censors', he called them, with no legal status whatsoever. No serious dramatist could work under these conditions, subjected to regulations on the use of certain words and subjects. Make your film, he added, and let the MPPA ban it, if they dare.

Leslie Howard, who had been given the part of Professor Higgins, was hopelessly wrong, he said – fatally wrong. The public would like him and would possibly expect him to marry Eliza, which was just what Shaw did *not* want.

Nevertheless he went on to describe what Leslie Howard should wear as Higgins – a cylindrical topper, badly in need of brushing, stuck on the back of his head; the black frock-coat of a professor; and a black overcoat, both these garments to be unvaleted. That would make him stand out in the crowd as a unique figure. Shaw wanted this get-up to be used again in the final scene.

In fact Leslie Howard did not dress like that; he wore a Shetland wool suit and a trilby hat: 'his conception', Wendy says, 'of the shaggy image of an Englishman. Leslie Howard was of Austrian origin, I think – his father's name was Frederick Stainer.'

Shaw enclosed a picture cut out of *The Listener,* illustrating an article by Compton Mackenzie about the period. That, he told Pascal, is exactly what Eliza should wear – hat and feathers, shawl, apron, and just that sort of basket.

From the very earliest stages of the preparation of the film Shaw was delighted with Wendy Hiller's performance. As early as the 18th November 1937, he wrote to Pascal: 'She will be the film sensation of the next five years. There is a fortune in her.'

A few days later he sent Wendy this letter, referring to a gift which she thought Shaw had been instrumental in sending her:

'My dear Wendy – don't believe Pascal: it is *his* present; but he is a modest creature and thought it would please you more if he said it came from me. I am a grabber, not a giver. Still, you have all the good wishes of mine that he put in the box; and it was handsome of him to pay for it.

'He sent me some stills of you from the studio. Superb. You will go over all the Hollywood charmers like a wet sponge over a full slate – G Bernard Shaw.'

Just before the shooting of the film Shaw and his wife were asked to a lunch at Pinewood Studios. He thought it would be just a simple affair, mainly for the cast, the director, and a few others, but found that more than a hundred guests had been invited, with Press reporters and a call for speeches. He was not prepared for this. When asked to address the assembly, Shaw rose to his great height and said simply: 'Ladies and gentlemen, the toast is Shaw!' and sat down.

Though he watched the shooting of only the first few scenes, Shaw kept in the closest touch with Gabriel Pascal at every stage of its progress. Any attempts by the cast to alter or adjust the interpretation of their parts made him furious and he told Pascal that no tinkering of any sort would be tolerated. In all only three of the new scenes written by Shaw for the film were used: they were the Bathroom scene, the Ballroom scene, and a scene outside the house, in which Eliza and Freddy are seen courting, and running away when the policeman appears.

Leslie Howard had doubts about the film, just as Shaw had doubts about his being the right choice for the part of Higgins. The film was completed in the autumn of 1938, with the possibility of war just round the corner, a war delayed only by Neville Chamberlain's pact with Hitler at Munich. Shaw was reasonably well pleased with the film, certainly much more so than with the two versions of it put out by German and Dutch film-makers, who had tampered with the text to the intense annoyance of the author.

Press and public gave the picture an enthusiastic reception; it opened a vast fresh avenue of triumphant opportunity for Shaw, by now in his eighty-third year. But his financial reward from it, though eventually quite large, was contractually complicated in its sequence of payments. On the completion of the film, Henry Andrews, the banker and husband of Rebecca West, who had a financial interest in the picture, saw the rough-cut and suggested certain small but important improvements. As this would involve the expenditure of a further sum of money, he offered to foot the bill, which ran into some thousands; and the contract provided that his share of the profits would take precedence over the others. When the film was ready for public showing Shaw asked Henry Andrews and Rebecca West to lunch and in the course of the meal told Andrews that he was extremely worried about a surtax demand for £3,000 which he had just received from the Tax Commissioners and was unable to meet. Andrews was surprised because Shaw was a man of immense means by this time; nevertheless, in order to allay his anxiety, Andrews said, 'You take the £3,000 now and after that the contract can take its course.' At this Shaw produced a typed sheet from his pocket and asked Andrews if he would call at the Mayfair Hotel on his way home and hand it to Gabriel Pascal. 'You see,' Shaw explained, 'Pascal had told me to be very firm with you and this note will indicate to him that all is well.' Andrews was annoyed that pressure should have been employed on him by this trick; but he said nothing to Shaw and, on leaving, drove to the Mayfair with the note.

A few minutes after Andrews and Rebecca had left the flat Shaw phoned a friend and said: 'Rebecca West is married to some City shark, who has been trying to do me out of my share of the profits from *Pygmalion*.' This was later repeated to Rebecca, who was understandably very angry, as Shaw and she had been friends for many years.

It was only a year or so before that Rebecca had asked me to a lunch at her flat in London to which Shaw had also been invited. Just before he was due to arrive she had a telephone call to say that he had a bad cold and was unable to come. She had prepared a special vegetarian lunch for him. She, her husband, Pat Wallace (Edgar Wallace's daughter) and I sat down to a normal lunch without Shaw.

A previous lunch for him at Rebecca's had met with disaster from a cause to which Shaw had in no way contributed. A large range of vegetarian dishes had been prepared for him by her highly skilled cook: they were varied and looked deliciously appetising. While the guest was awaited, the cook, who suffered from *petit mal,* had a sudden attack; on recovering, she blinked at the dishes around her in the kitchen and concluded that the oncoming attack had caused her to forget to put any meat or fish in them. Quickly she repaired her oversight. When the food was brought to the table and served to Shaw, he was not only appalled but angry. He seemed to feel it was part of a plot to force him to depart from his strict vegetarian diet. That Rebecca was horrified at what had happened did not appear to assuage him in the slightest. He went on growling and grumbling; his denunciation knew no bounds. He refused to remain at the table. Rebecca, remarking that it was not of the slightest interest to her whether he remained a vegetarian or not, went into the kitchen and under her supervision a fresh range of vegetarian dishes were prepared. His smile returned as he sat down again at the table, but the atmosphere he had created could not be dispelled quite so easily.

Pascal's resolve to follow *Pygmalion* with the filming of another of Shaw's plays led eventually to the selection of *Major Barbara,* a play about the Salvation Army.

Once again Wendy Hiller was selected for the leading role. But having embarked on her first engagement at a very modest salary – she received well under £1,000 for eight weeks' work – she asked if the fee could be improved. But Pascal demurred and Shaw felt it necessary to intervene.

Writing to Pascal on the 26th August 1938 from the Impney Hotel at Droitwich, the Worcestershire spa, Shaw told him not to quarrel with Wendy, who either had a good adviser or a good business head of her own: in her place he would behave exactly in that way. He wanted Wendy to appear in further films of his and had already earmarked her for the role of St Joan.

Pascal had suggested that a film should be made of *Candida* and that Katherine Cornell should play the leading role. But Shaw would not have it. *Candida* was one of her trump cards on the stage and to film it would kill the play stone dead, which would not be a good thing either for Katherine Cornell or for Shaw. Besides, the length of the play was two hours without a change of scene. It is not suitable for the cinema, he added, because there is no visual interest.

That letter had its effect and all was settled satisfactorily. Wendy was given the title-role in *Major Barbara* and the film version went into production. Rex Harrison, who was later to play Professor Higgins in the musical stage and film version of *Pygmalion*, made in America and re-titled *My Fair Lady*, played Wendy's young admirer in *Major Barbara*. As Adolphus Cusins, an Oxford Professor of Greek (based largely on Gilbert Murray, the Greek scholar and translator), he was required to wear glasses and talk as an intellectual with a subtle sense of humour and an appalling temper at the slightest hint of ridicule. Shaw, more amenable now to the persuasive wiles of Pascal, agreed to shorten the play by cutting out certain scenes and even wrote sixteen fresh sequences of which only six were used; in one of these we saw Rex Harrison overcome by a glass of vodka – Gilbert Murray, who had recognised himself, did not like this drunken scene. Robert Morley played the stoutish elderly Andrew Undershaft; Deborah Kerr, who later won world fame in Hollywood, played little Jenny Hill, a pale, overwrought but pretty Salvation Army lass; Sybil Thorndike and Emlyn Williams were others in that striking cast.

The rehearsals, at which Shaw was present, provided some amusing moments. Both Rex Harrison and Wendy Hiller told me of their inability to make much sense of the 'Oh, for the wings of a dove' speech at the end of the last act.

'I talked to Pascal about it,' Rex told me, 'and together we approached Shaw and asked if he would explain it to us. He took the script into a corner where he sat with his head in his hands and read it silently. When he had finished he said: "Oh what a terrible scene! Did I write that?" But he wouldn't alter the scene. He said: "I have no right to touch the play – it's a classic!"'

'Some of our rehearsals were held in the Albert Hall,' Rex added, 'and Shaw had some wonderfully funny ideas for the trombone and tambourines and other instruments of the Salvation Army band. He kept hopping about with trombone and tambourine and improvised quite hilarious moments which were really most effective .'

The shooting of the film did not begin until after the outbreak of the Second World War. In the early months Dartington Hall in Devon was used for the production – they were still shooting there at the time of Dunkirk – and the film was not ready to be shown to the public until the end of 1941. Film-goers in England were delighted with it; and in America, despite the scant interest there in the Salvation Army, it was an even bigger success: the trailer, in which Shaw talked about the film, appealed to them enormously. He had made only one previous appearance in a film when he talked for a few minutes before a Movietone camera in his own home in the country.

As was to be expected, Shaw clowned, saying he looked like Mussolini, but was able to discard his frown whereas Mussolini could not; whereupon he not only smiled, but beamed at the audience. The *Major Barbara* trailer, which he and some friends went to see at a local country cinema, led him to observe in an aside to his secretary: 'Now watch – and you will see my teeth come down.' Miss Patch watched nervously, but his dentures fortunately remained in position; Shaw could never avoid his little joke.

The making by Pascal of his third and final film, *Caesar and Cleopatra*, with Vivien Leigh, Claude Rains, Stewart Granger and Michael Rennie as stars, took some years to complete. Its cost was phenomenal for an English film at that time; it ran far above the scheduled budget of under half a million pounds and reached the astonishing total of £1,300,000. Pascal's extravagance in his quest for exactitude, as he called it, knew no bounds. He had an enormous Sphinx built in the studio at Denham, then dismantled it and sent the players and the entire film unit to Egypt so that they would have the actual desert sands, studded with real palm trees, to gallop across. More sand was purchased in England for the making of a desert in the studio, and a harbour wall was built rising high above the trees in the park so that Caesar and the others could jump from it into the sea, which had also to be provided. Once again Shaw, who had come to recognise that the screen required continuous movement, agreed to cuts in the text of his play and added fresh linking scenes to provide a flow to the story.

Although by this time he was nearly ninety, Shaw went to the studio from time to time to see how the shooting, and more particularly the acting, were progressing; but he relied for the most part on the weekly visits from Pascal, who called at Ayot St Lawrence with 'stills', and gave a report on what was happening. Queen Mary attended the première at the Odeon at Marble Arch, but the traffic jam was so great that Pascal arrived too late to be presented to her.

By now Shaw had reached the closing years of his life, but before we turn to them, let us look at two important journeys made by him to Russia and China.

12
To Russia and China

SHAW WAS IN his seventy-fifth year when he went to
Russia; he had been invited by the Soviet Government
because a number of his plays, in particular *The Apple
Cart*, had enjoyed considerable success there, and many
had heard of his dedication to Communism. He accepted
the invitation with alacrity and asked if he could bring
a party of friends with him. The Soviet's response was
favourable and he chose his companions from members
of the Conservative Party and the aristocracy – Lady
Astor, who was a Conservative Member of Parliament,
the first woman ever to take her seat in the House of
Commons, her husband the very rich Viscount Astor,
their son David Astor, who was then nineteen years old,
the Marquess of Lothian, and Charles Tennant, a
Christian Scientist who was to become Lord Glenconner
– an odd assembly for the Communists to welcome.

They travelled by train in July 1931 and were joined
in the dining-car of the Berlin–Moscow express by
Litvinoff, the Commissar for Foreign Affairs. A vast
crowd at Moscow station cheered wildly as they saw the
tall, slender, magnificently erect old man with a white
beard alight from the railway carriage. A guard of
honour had been drawn up and a brass band enlivened
his welcome; no notice was taken of the other members
of the party. Reporters, photographers with flashing
bulbs, prominent Russian authors and members of the
Soviet Foreign Office gathered round him and Shaw was
delighted: the reception surpassed all his expectations.
As he drove off, a crowd numbering many thousands

waved their banners and sent up a mighty cheer. The best room in the Metropole Hotel had been reserved for him; the Astors had a small one on the top floor.

His nine-day stay in Russia began with the declaration, 'I was a Socialist before Lenin was born'. The Mausoleum in Red Square in which Lenin, who had died seven years before, lay embalmed in a glass case, was visited by Shaw, who also insisted on visiting Lenin's widow, Krupskaya, in her villa in the country. She said little but appeared to be very flattered by his coming to see her. He also went to the Kremlin on Stalin's invitation and talked to the Red dictator, a privilege denied to almost all visitors; but he had to promise not to mention this while still in Russia. Stalin, dressed in uniform and long boots, talked with Shaw for more than an hour: what was said Shaw summarised on his return to England: 'Stalin asked why Churchill was so anti-Russia. I said he had a "bee in his bonnet" and was hopelessly old-fashioned. But Stalin was not satisfied with this reply. He has a high opinion of Mr Churchill's ability. We told him that he need not worry, because Churchill would probably lose his seat at the next election and anyhow would never be Prime Minister.' Shaw was wrong, of course, for Churchill not only retained his seat in Parliament at the election less than three months later, but became Prime Minister in less than nine years. After the talk, the Press pursued Shaw to his hotel and up the stairs to his room; but Shaw would say nothing. Just before entering his room Shaw turned and faced his questioners. 'You want to know what happened. Well, I'll tell you. We discovered that Stalin has a big black moustache.'

For Shaw's seventy-fifth birthday on the 26th July, Stalin arranged a large and impressive reception. Feeling exhilarated on orange juice, Shaw let himself go in a speech of gay and irresponsible exaggeration. He said that the relatives of those who had come with him to Russia had wept and clung to them begging them not to go as they would certainly die there of starvation. 'We brought away large parcels and baskets of food, bedding and even tents, so as to make sure of having a roof over our heads. But the moment the train crossed your border, we saw our mistake and dropped everything out of the carriage window.' Then, pointing to the Astors, Lord Lothian and his other companions he described them as capitalists and rich landowners. 'You mustn't blame them,' he added, 'they can't alter the system, but the British proletariat will alter it.' The party were taken to a race meeting where Shaw was so bored that he fell asleep in the grandstand, while Lady Astor fanned him to keep off the flies.

Back from Russia Shaw declared that the Soviet Union was the nearest place in the world to an earthly paradise. Winston Churchill pronounced the last word about the trip. Writing in the *Sunday Pictorial* (now the *Sunday Mirror*) he said: 'Mr Bernard Shaw is at once a wealthy and acquisitive capitalist and a sincere Communist. His spiritual home is Russia, but he lives comfortably in England. He couples the possession of a mild, amiable and humane disposition with the advocacy and even glorification of the vilest political crimes and cruelties. He indulges all the liberties of an irresponsible chatterbox babbling from dawn to dusk. He has laughed his sparkling way through life, exploding by his own acts or words every argument he has ever used on either side in any question, teasing and bewildering every public he has addressed, and involving in mockery and discredit every cause he has ever championed.'

Shaw's visit to China took place nearly two years later, in 1933; it was part of a round-the-world trip which took him to India, Hong Kong, on to Japan and across the Pacific to Hollywood and eventually to New York.

He defined his attitude to Communism in a speech to the Chinese students at Hong Kong University – China was not at that time Communist, though it had a Communist party. 'If at twenty,' Shaw told them, 'you don't join the Reds in their revolution, you'll become fossils at fifty.' This was strongly resented by a great many people on the island and was severely attacked by the Press. Leaving the ship at Shanghai, he received at his hotel some of the most prominent poets and playwrights of China; he also saw Madame Sun Yat-Sen, the widow of the great revolutionary who overthrew the Manchu dynasty in 1911. In a message to the people of China Shaw said: 'When her revolution is completed China will have achieved a complete cure for that disease called civilisation, either by changing it to her own benefit or rejecting it altogether. In the meantime I can only look on and wonder what is going to happen. It is not for me, belonging as I do to a quarter of the globe which is mismanaging its affairs in a ruinous fashion, to pretend to advise an ancient people desperately striving to set its house in order. Europe can give no counsel to Asia, except at the risk of the old rebuff "Physician heal thyself". I am afraid I have likewise nothing to say in the present emergency except "China help thyself". '

He visited one of the lovely islands of Hangchow, and signed his name in the visitors' book in the old pavilion, now a museum, where the poet Su Tung-po had once lived. From there he went on by train to Peking with Charlotte – a long, overnight journey.

His great love of the theatre took him to a play every night and often to matinées as well. Peking was neither clean nor sanitary at the time and Shaw picked up a germ in the crowded, suffocating theatre. It had no effect on him whatsoever. Charlotte, writing home to a friend, said: 'He gave the germ to me. I was very ill and had to stay in bed for a week.' But Shaw continued to go out night after night, with an interpreter seated beside him translating the Chinese operas, which at that time went on for six or seven hours.

On her recovery, Shaw insisted that Charlotte should go with him to see the Great Wall of China. The best way to see it, he decided, would be from an aeroplane, which would reveal the vast expanse of the long, rambling 2,000-year-old wall that had been erected as a barrier against the northern invaders.

Their plane was one of the early biplanes, their seats were open to the sky. As the plane flew low over the Great Wall Shaw was horrified to see just below them a fierce battle in progress between the Chinese army and a horde of armed Japanese, who had invaded Manchuria the year before and had been advancing southward in an effort to subjugate China – this they all but succeeded in doing during the years that followed.

Shaw frenziedly jabbed the shoulder of the pilot in front. 'Turn back. Turn back!' he shouted. 'I don't like wars. I don't want to look at this.' The biplane circled and took the Shaws back to Peking.

This flight at the age of seventy-seven was by no means his first. Always eager to test new things he had gone up in an aeroplane in England in 1912 when very few people were daring enough to trust their lives to planes – the First World War was two years away and it was not until its final year that aeroplanes were involved in combat on the Western Front. Even earlier, in 1906, tall and red-bearded then, he had gone up in a balloon.

When Lennox Robinson and I went to China in 1956 to take part in the Shaw centenary celebrations, the country had been Communist for seven years, following Mao Tse-Tung's victory in the long-drawn-out civil war against Chiang Kai-Shek. We kept ourselves completely aloof from politics and learned nothing of the stern measures that had been employed to transform the cities of that vast country into clean, orderly and modern towns of intense activity, with new factories, their roofs bearing echoes of the old traditional style of Chinese architecture, the people disciplined and docile and working in shifts for long hours, the women depositing their infants in the nursery annexes while they themselves laboured by day and by night.

We were asked to assist in planning a Shaw programme for the anniversary celebration in Peking. We found that acquaintance with his plays was slight; it was confined almost entirely to *Mrs Warren's Profession*, which puzzled us as China had abolished all brothels, but the play seemed to them to have some bearing on the liberation of their own women from the suffocating seclusion of the home. We could not steer them away from it. It was being acted by professionals and amateurs all over China and they insisted on it being included in the programme. In the end two scenes from it, performed by students from the Central Academy of Dramatic Art, were selected and played in Chinese. These, I suggested, should be preceded by the scene from *The Apple Cart* in which the American Ambassador tells King Magnus of England that his country wished to return to the English fold. The thought delighted them. The play had not yet been translated into Chinese, but although they had less than a week for making the translation and for rehearsals, it was adopted and the members of the Peking Cinema Actors' Troupe were word-perfect on the night of the performance. The Chinese girl who played the Queen was young and pretty and in her Western clothes and make-up could have passed for English. Her role did not demand much of her; in that scene she had just to sit and listen, but she used her feather fan most expressively, opening it and shutting it to indicate her reactions to what was being said by the King and the Ambassador.

The great ballroom of the Peking Hotel was packed to the doors; the entire diplomatic corps was present, including the British Chargé d'Affaires, Mr Con O'Neill, and his wife. After the performance of the excerpts from the plays, the speeches began. Though Shaw was being honoured, the Chinese speakers were critical of him, indicating that while his ideas were revolutionary he lacked the spirit to carry them out. Tien Han, Chairman of the Union of Chinese Stage Artists, quoting Lenin,

said: 'Shaw was a good man fallen among Fabians. . . .
But it was not until the Russian Revolution and the
appearance of the Soviet Socialist Republic that the
depression of the old playwright became dispersed. So he
ended by saying, "We are Socialists. Russia's viewpoint
is also ours." ' At that time China was a dedicated
admirer of Russia's form of Communism.

Lennox Robinson and I spoke in English, with an
interpreter at our elbow to translate the speeches,
sentence by sentence. Lennox spoke of his association
with Shaw, as his secretary, and also about Shaw's plays.
I could not resist getting in this little jibe. 'I remember
when England was honouring Shakespeare on the three-
hundredth anniversary of his death, Bernard Shaw was
invited to join in the tributes. He had to travel only a
hundred miles to Shakespeare's birthplace at Stratford-
on-Avon, but he refused to go. None the less he would
have been delighted that two men he knew, one from
England and the other from his own birthplace Ireland,
should have come many thousands of miles, travelling
continuously in aeroplanes, tossed across the skies from
Finland to Russia, Mongolia to China, bumped up and
down and often without sleep, just to honour Shaw. That,
he would have said, is as it should be.'

There were numerous other Shaw celebrations – at
Shanghai, where the whole of his *Arms and the Man* was
acted in Chinese, in Manchuria and elsewhere, at each of
which we were called upon to talk of him and his plays.

13

His Closing Years

On his wife's death Shaw, who was eighty-seven, asked
Mrs Alice Laden, who had nursed her, if she would come
and look after him at his home at Ayot St Lawrence,
where he proposed to live in future.

Mrs Laden, who knew the house and did not like it,
hated even more the thought of living in the country. 'I
am a town-woman,' she told me. 'I have never cared for a
country life. There were no buses or trams at Ayot, the
entire population of which numbered less than one
hundred. The nearest shopping centre, Welwyn, was about
five miles away, very few tradesmen called and, as Mr
Shaw himself indicated quite frankly at this interview,
there was no cinema in the village, no Woolworth's and
very little else. I realised I would be completely cut off
and was about to refuse his offer, but he looked at me so
pathetically that I hesitated about giving him a blank
refusal. I said I did not much like the thought of being
buried in the country. "Don't give me your answer now,"
he said. "Think about it, and I very much hope you will
say yes. You can see I need you." I was touched by his
plea, but I could not see myself going to live at Ayot. I
agreed, however, to think it over and I hoped in the
meantime he would find someone else.

'Within a matter of hours I was offered a most remun-
erative job as a housekeeper at Whitehall Court. It
involved looking after the large number of flats that
comprise that vast block. I mentioned what Mr Shaw
had said and was told that I would find it extremely
trying to work for that "rude" and "irascible" old man. I

bridled at this. I certainly had found him neither rude nor irascible. That put me off accepting the White-hall Court offer. Anyway, I needed a rest after my long spell of nursing Mrs Shaw. Towards the end her hands were badly swollen and I had to feed her and do a large number of other things for her. So I told Mr Shaw that I had decided to go to Scotland and would let him know whether I would be able to come back to him.'

While she was away he sent her a number of further appeals. 'I felt he wanted me because I provided a link with his wife, and there would thus be some continuity in his way of life. At the same time I was only too conscious of the many grave disadvantages, for apart from living in relative isolation, I knew that the house at Ayot was in a very bad state of repair. Would Mr Shaw be prepared to do anything about that? I doubted that a man of his advanced age, and with his sense of money, would be ready to pour out quite a large sum on house repairs and redecoration.'

Shaw meanwhile was taking it for granted that Mrs Laden would be coming to him, for he wrote in a letter to Lady Astor with his customary exaggeration and sense of fun: 'Ha! Ha! Mrs Laden is coming as a house-keeper for me. She has gone to her shooting lodge in Scotland. And who knows, I might end up by marrying her.' At any rate the first part of his forecast proved to be correct, for Mrs Laden, after considerable reflection, decided to go and look after him, and, to his delight, she arrived at Ayot St Lawrence shortly afterwards, took charge of the house and reorganised its running to minister to his way of life.

'The house was not easy to run,' she says. 'It was an old Victorian house – actually two houses joined to-gether. It had been used as the rectory when there were two churches in the village – Ayot St Peter and Ayot St Lawrence – but the population kept diminishing and the rectory, which was much too large, was no longer required.'

The Shaws, who had been moving from house to house

for some years to find somewhere to settle, only rented it as a temporary makeshift. But they got used to it in time and bought the house just after the First World War. Its name, 'The Old Rectory', was retained, but shortly after Mrs Laden joined him, on deciding to bequeath the house to the National Trust, Shaw changed its name to 'Shaw's Corner' and inscribed this in large letters on a wrought-iron superstructure above the gateway. The simple plain gates, which met in the middle when closed, were replaced at the same time by a large white one.

Shortly after moving in, Mrs Laden told him that the house had been sadly neglected and needed to be completely redecorated. To this Shaw readily agreed. Mr Almond, the builder in the adjoining village of Codicot, was brought in, and Shaw gave him his orders. 'I want you to do the job exactly as Mrs Laden wants it done. I don't want any estimates. Just allow yourself a good profit.' The work cost £1,000, and he didn't quibble over the bill.

The question of having new curtains was then raised. The existing curtains were old and shabby, Mrs Laden pointed out. Something had to be done about them now that the house was looking so nice. Shaw looked at her with narrowed eyes. 'I'm a poor man, Mrs Laden,' he said. This was a setback and Mrs Laden felt it would be wiser to play for time. 'I'll talk to you when you are in a different mood,' she said. In the end he gave way and new curtains were put up.

'I really was very happy to be with him. I got used to Ayot and he got used to me. There was a staff of two maids, one an Irish girl called Maggie, the other was an English girl, Violet. He also had a chauffeur for his Rolls-Royce and there was another car, an old chocolate-coloured Lanchester, which was mainly for the staff's use. The chauffeur did the gardening, though Mr Shaw did quite a bit of pottering about himself, cutting down low branches of trees, trimming the hedges and chopping

148

wood for three-quarters of an hour every afternoon by way of exercise.

'As the war was still on when I joined him, early in 1944, I had to handle not only his and my ration books but also those of the entire staff – food and clothes rationing went on for some years after the war, and I had to deal with all their cards. Mr Shaw discussed the question of the housekeeping money with me. He always changed his cheques, he said, at the butcher's. I asked him if he wanted me to do that too or did he think it might be better if I used a nearby bank. He replied, "I'll think it over." He was like that; although he was always quick with his public announcements, he liked turning things over in his mind before coming to a decision that concerned him. A day or two later he broached the subject himself. He began by asking the name of my bank. I told him. He said: "My account is at the Oxford Street branch of the Westminster Bank. I'm going to open an account in your name at the Wheathamstead branch of that bank, and I shall place a few hundred pounds there for your use." When I next went to London I called at his bank (as Mr Shaw had asked me to do) to see that his instructions were being carried out. The bank manager stared at me, then with a note of intense surprise, he said: "I have never known him do that before."

'Mr Shaw, as is well known, was a vegetarian. He had not always been, so I understand.' It was not in fact until he was twenty-five that Shaw gave up eating meat; that was five years after he came to London. 'I was a cannibal,' he wrote. 'It was Shelley who first opened my eyes to the savagery of my diet.' At that time in desperate financial straits, eating in one of the many vegetarian restaurants then being opened in London made the change not only cheaper but practicable. He later described himself as a 'living proof that neither fish, flesh nor fowl is indispensable to success in life and literature'. His will, he declared, 'contains directions for

149

my funeral, which will be followed not by mourning coaches but by herds of oxen, sheep, swine, flocks of poultry and a small travelling aquarium of live fish, all wearing white scarves in honour of the man who perished rather than eat his fellow creatures'.

Mrs Laden took over the preparing and cooking of his vegetarian meals. Already a highly skilled cook, she was anxious now to acquire as wide a knowledge as possible of preparing vegetarian dishes. She found there was a school of vegetarian cooking in Marylebone Road in London and went there two mornings a week for several months and was thus able to provide Shaw with a greater variety of dishes than he had ever had before.

'He was not as fond of his food as Mrs Shaw. The quantity she consumed at each meal was really astonishing. What Mr Shaw used to do was to linger over his meals. He liked soft messy dishes and would not allow me to cook any of the vegetables. He preferred to eat them raw with dollops of mango chutney on them.

'Breakfast was served to him punctually at seven o'clock every morning. He came down fully dressed, having risen at six am, washed and gone through his series of physical jerks. He went straight into the dining-room and began with grapefruit, both halves of which had been lavishly sugared. This was followed by toast, butter and marmalade. No tea – he never drank tea: it was always just a glass of milk. Often this was followed by fruit – fresh fruit. I was surprised that he had no soft fruit such as strawberries, raspberries and red currants growing in the garden. There were apple trees and pear trees, but most of the other fruit was bought.

'His breakfast was lingered over for two and a half hours. He remained in the dining-room till the newspapers were delivered at about nine o'clock – he took the Communist paper *The Daily Worker*, the Socialist *Daily Herald* and *The Times* – and he read them until the post arrived and was handed to him by the maid. The mail was always very heavy – at times quite colossal – and generally there were many parcels, mostly gifts from admirers in all parts of the world. He insisted on opening all the letters himself and had a paper-knife by his elbow to slit open the envelopes. The important ones he replied to at once, using his little cards with his name and address at the top for some, and large sheets of his notepaper for others – every one was written by hand. The letters were then inserted in their envelopes, which he licked down and placed on a newspaper spread out on the floor, he stuck on the stamps himself and took the newspaper with its load of letters into the hall for one of the maids to take to the post. The other letters were set aside for the time being.

'Punctually at ten o'clock he left the dining-room and walked to the far end of his garden to the hut in which he worked. It stood by a wood which Mrs Shaw had planted for him to provide a buffer for his privacy. The small alarm-clock on the table was set for one o'clock so that he would know when it was time to return for lunch. The hut was on a revolving base so that it could be turned to get the sun while he was writing. A small electric fire was used in the winter. His plays were written in shorthand and sent to his secretary in Whitehall Court in London to be typed. On the typewriter he tapped out his instructions to me or to his secretary, and sometimes he typed his personal letters to Sidney Webb and his other friends.

'When the alarm went off he put his pen down and walked back to the house, with time enough to wash and tidy up before going in to lunch at 1.15. Later when he reached the age of ninety he was inclined to fall asleep; a house-phone was installed so that I could ring up and tell him that lunch was about to be served.'

Nearly two hours were spent over lunch. At three o'clock he dealt briefly with the less important letters, scribbling on them what he wanted his secretary to write in reply. Then he stretched himself out on the sofa in the dining-room and went to sleep until 4.30. No one dared disturb him: he took no telephone calls and refused to receive any visitors, however important. There was a bed in the garden-hut and he sometimes slept there after lunch in the summer.

'He was very methodical, his routine never varied. On awakening at 4.30 he would put on a hat – he had a great variety of hats – sling one of his many cameras over his shoulder, take a stick and go out for a walk – he never went for a walk without his camera. Just before six o'clock he returned, except on those occasions when, while walking through the village, he wandered into the church and got lost in meditation. The six o'clock news was an important part of his day and he rarely missed it by being out too long.'

More work followed. As soon as the news ended he went back to the hut. He had a new play in preparation, *Buoyant Billions*, and began to write it in 1946 when he was ninety. It took two years to complete. He wanted it to be performed at Malvern, where the annual Festival had been suspended while the war was on: but the theatre was to be reopened there as soon as certain structural alterations had been carried out. These took longer than expected and the play had its first production in Zürich under the title *Zu Viel Geld*. While it was being written a curious pressman asked Shaw what the title of the new play was to be. He replied: 'It has not been finally decided. Provisionally I am calling it *Piffle*.' It was a full-length play in four acts. Unfortunately it was not a good play, but much of the old fire was still noticeable in the dialogue. For instance, when Miss Buoyant tells her solicitor friend: 'The day of ridiculous old maids is over. Great men have been bachelors and great women virgins,' he replies: 'They may have regretted it all the same. Celibacy for a woman is *il gran rifiuto*, the great refusal, of her destiny, of the purpose of life which comes before all personal considerations: the replacing of the dead by the living' – by which, he meant, of course, motherhood. When the play was published in book-form Shaw stated in his preface: 'As long as I live I must write.

152

If I stopped writing I should die for want of something to do.' And he went on writing. In 1949, when he was ninety-three, he wrote *Farfetched Fables*, a short light book, and also published *Sixteen Self Sketches*, most of which was autobiographical. Then followed a puppet-play called *Shakes versus Shaw*. This done, he began work, at the age of ninety-four, on his fifty-eighth and last play. Tentatively called *X*, it was later given the title *Why She Would Not*. He never finished it.

After an hour in the hut writing, following the six o'clock news, Shaw came in and changed from his Norfolk jacket, knickerbockers and brogue shoes to a black suit – still with knickerbockers (not long trousers) – and went in to dinner, which was a light meal consisting of soup, a compote of fresh fruit and cream, rounded off by very white coffee.

'Though the meal may seem slight,' says Mrs Laden, 'he had a very good appetite. I served him with large quantities of everything. He stayed in the dining-room after the meal: he never used the drawing-room. Mrs Shaw had furnished it, but he did not like it at all. The radio was put on at about 9.15 and he listened to the Third Programme most of the evening, or he would read. He wouldn't have a television set in the house. "It's bad enough listening to them, without having to see them as well," he used to say. There were large boxes of sweets and chocolates beside him, and he kept on munching them until it was time to go to bed. Sometimes, on one pretext or another, he would ring for one the maids and say he would like to see me. His purpose actually was to talk. He wasn't really a lonely man; he liked being by himself. But some memory of the past would stir him to communicate it to a listener and I was the recipient. Mostly he talked of his childhood or his marriage or his friends. He was always most amusing. Once he asked me if I was happy in my married life. I said: "Yes, but unfortunately it was short." He commented: "I can't imagine how two people *can* be happy." "They are," I

153

replied. "Most people are not," he said, "but they are not honest enough to admit it. Marriage is a peculiar relationship." '

Shaw didn't go to the theatre now, but if a play of his was revived he sent Mrs Laden in the car to see it and waited eagerly for her return, often well after midnight, to ply her with questions about the acting, the setting and the audience. One of his earlier plays, *You Never Can Tell,* written sixty years before and which had to wait four years for a Stage Society performance, had his particular affection. 'It did very well later and I was always glad to have it resuscitated when I needed money.' In October 1947 it was revived at Wyndham's Theatre with Jane Henderson in the rôle of Mrs Clandon. 'I went to see it,' Mrs Laden told me, 'and I liked it very much. Mr Shaw asked me no end of questions. "Tell me about the clothes the leading lady wore," he asked. I described Jane Henderson's dress. It was grey with black stripes, a close-fitting bodice and a long skirt. Her hat was flat, off-white in colour and trimmed with chiffon, with white bird's wings across the front, and tied under the chin. On hearing this Mr Shaw exploded. "I waste my time writing plays for them and they wear what they like," he said. "Ring up Lady Astor and ask her to send me a three-cornered cocked hat – it must be three-cornered and it must be black – she is always wearing that sort of hat in the House of Commons." I phoned her and she said she had one that she no longer wore, and sent it to us. Mr Shaw examined it and approved of it. I then packed it carefully and the chauffeur took it to the theatre with Mr Shaw's instructions that Miss Henderson had to wear that hat. An hour later Mr Shaw phoned to the theatre himself and talked to the actress about it, insisting that that was the hat she was to wear.

'I had quite a dispute with Mr Shaw one day about the dining-room carpet; it had a large hole in it and I told him that, as he always entertained his friends in that room, he ought to get a new one, because his visitors

154

sometimes caught their feet in the hole. He gave me the answer I always expected to get: "I am a poor man, Mrs Laden. I cannot afford a new carpet." Quite bluntly I said: "I am not listening to that. Will you allow me to go to Hampton's and see what I can get at a very reasonable price?" After much persuasion, spread out over many talks, he at last agreed and set the limit of £300 to £350 as the price I was to pay. But I did a lot better than that. I saw in *The Times* Personal column that somebody had a Persian carpet for sale. I went down to Cobham in Surrey to look at it. It was just the right size, and the colours were most attractive, with blue predominating. Mr Shaw had signed a blank cheque and I filled in the sum, which was only 95 guineas. When I handed the cheque to the woman, she looked at the name. "Oh! Bernard Shaw!" she said. She appeared nevertheless to be in some doubt as to whether it was really Bernard Shaw's cheque; so she phoned the bank to make sure. When I returned home in his Lanchester, Mr Shaw was in the hut, and Day, his chauffeur-gardener, and I together laid it down on the dining-room floor. When he came in and saw it he was delighted. "She has given it away – given it away to you," he said when I told him the price.'

It was never easy to get Shaw up to bed. He stayed in the dining-room till well after midnight. 'Often,' says Mrs Laden, 'I used to find him asleep in a chair in the dining-room. He would wake up quickly when I came in and say "Yes?" I told him he would be much more comfortable if he went to bed. "My mother never went to bed before midnight," he said, "and I don't see why I should." I always went round last thing at night to make sure that all the doors were firmly fastened. But to my distress he used to go into the kitchen last thing at night and unfasten the back door in order to breathe in the fresh night air before retiring, and often he would forget to fasten it again. I don't know how many times I had to talk to him about it. "Don't you realise," I would say, "that one of these nights burglars will come in through the kitchen door and make a clean sweep of everything that's worth taking?" He'd just brush off my chiding. "I forgot – and no burglars came anyway." It made me so cross. There had been a number of burglaries in the neighbourhood. "Well, don't forget next time," I'd say. His reply was that of a naughty boy. "I can't promise. I may do it again." – "Then you ought to go to bed at a reasonable time. You can't expect me to keep awake and go round the house after you."

'It just went on night after night. I used to prowl about and wait till he left the dining-room to see that the doors were locked. He caught me at this one night and came down the stairs again "What are you up to?" he asked. "Why aren't you in bed?" I said. He chuckled: "You'll find I've locked everything"; but he hadn't – the dining-room door was locked, but the back door had been left wide open and the garden light was on so that the burglars could see that the door was open. Another thing I was afraid of was that he might set fire to the place. He didn't smoke, of course, but he used to write sometimes in the evenings and warmed a cushion by the fire. There was a stool by the stove and the cushion was put on it. One night it fell off the stool and caught fire. Smelling smoke, I came hurrying down and found the attractive red velvet top of the stool and its entire stuffing ablaze. "If I hadn't come back the whole house would have been burned down," I said. He just looked at me sheepishly.

'And when he did go to bed that wasn't the end of my problems. Quite often at about two or three o'clock in the morning we would all be awakened by the sound of the piano being played – it stood at the foot of the stairs and could be heard all over the house. It was impossible to go to sleep again while he was strumming away down there. Mostly he would be playing Mozart and Beethoven – and he played well, I must say. But after a time he would strike up a music-hall ditty and bellow it out at the top of his voice. It is really remarkable what a large number of the old music-hall songs he knew. Irish songs were brought in sometimes – the old songs and very lovely some of them were – but we didn't want to be awakened from sleep in the small hours of the morning to listen to them.'

14
His Visitors

ONE OF MRS Laden's most important tasks was to fend off the shoals of visitors who hovered round the house and peered through the hedges just to catch a glimpse of Shaw. In addition to these prying sightseers there were large numbers of others who came boldly up to the front door, rang the bell and announced that they were Shaw's relatives, who had come from New Zealand or Australia or Canada to see him. 'I always scrutinised their features most closely,' Mrs Laden told me, 'to see if there was the slightest flicker of a resemblance. If there was not I drove them off and didn't even inform Mr Shaw. The real relatives – and there were a few – would not have dropped in without warning.

'I also had to cope with the Press. They came at frequent intervals, bringing their notebooks to record every casual remark he made, while cameras were cocked and bulbs flashed liked lightning. Every birthday was an ordeal. Mr Shaw never minded being photographed, in fact he loved it, but to be pounced on suddenly was distracting and disturbing; it kept him from his work – the books and plays he wanted to finish writing.'

At the very outset Shaw told Mrs Laden that she would have to be the dragon in his life and protect him from all intruders. 'They came in swarms at times, not just in ones and twos. It was a continuous pilgrimage. I seemed hardly ever to be away from that front door. As soon as I left it there would be a face at one of the windows, or peeping through the hedge, or a group of men, women and even children coming through the gate.

It had to be dealt with quite firmly and I used to shout: "Go away! Mr Shaw can't see you!" and if they still hung about I would warn them: "If you don't go away in two minutes I'll throw a bucket of hot water over you." Sometimes this scared them and they went. But others wouldn't budge, they just stayed on and started arguing. They answered back and occasionally were offensive. When the altercation became very heated Mr Shaw would rush out of the dining-room brandishing his thick stick and roaring like a lion. One persistent young man with a camera took a snapshot of him like this and sent him the picture. Many complaints about me were sent to Mr Shaw. He always sent the same reply. "If I didn't have Mrs Laden, I'd have to keep a ferocious Alsatian dog. You have no idea what it is to be a celebrity."

'He told me one day, "You are here as a dragon and that's exactly what I want you to be. I have bought you this" – and he opened a small box he had in his hand. Inside was a dragon brooch. "This is your badge of office," he said. I wear it to this day.

'I had also to be a dragon on the telephone. It scarcely ever stopped ringing. Although he kept his number out of the phone book, he very thoughtlessly put it on his notepaper as well as on the numerous postcards he sent, many of them to total strangers. As these letters and cards came on to the market, his telephone number became quite widely known. The calls included a great many from people who wanted him to open bazaars, fêtes and garden-parties, or to speak at public dinners, or to make appointments to see them, most of whom he had never heard of. The moment the phone rang he would shout from the dining-room, "I don't want to talk to anyone, alive or dead," and I had to convey this as politely as I could to the caller. "If such pests," Mr Shaw once told me, "existed in Shakespeare's day his literary output would have been much reduced, and we would not have had twenty of his most famous plays.

159

They would never have been written." '

But not all the callers were unwanted. Shaw was always pleased to see his friends. One of the more frequent of these visitors was Nancy Astor. They had known each other since 1927 (Shaw was then seventy-one) and remained close friends till the end of his life. American by birth, beautiful as a girl, she had posed as a model for the artist Charles Dana Gibson, who was married to her sister Irene; after divorcing her first husband, Robert Shaw, Nancy married Lord Astor, and settled in England. Shaw always said that he was first drawn to her when, after listening in the House to a speech with which she disagreed, she shouted, 'Rats!' It was her blunt and unequivocal manner of saying what she thought that attracted him. She was quick with her retorts, and these two were able to spark off each other. Politically they were at opposite ends of the pole, for she was a Conservative, but she agreed with some of the reforms he advocated and was as vigorously opposed to the consumption of alcohol as he was; and it is not far-fetched to say that they got on so well because they intoxicated each other with their banter. She got him to be Santa Claus at a party at her home, Cliveden, on the Thames, given for her household staff and their families. 'You look like Santa Claus,' she said in her invitation to him, 'even though you have the manners of the Devil.' He sometimes appeared among her elegant guests on Cliveden's lordly terrace dressed in his customary costume – Norfolk jacket, knickerbockers and stockings, and a cloth cap. On another occasion, when she asked him to her constituency at Plymouth, to open a hostel given to the University College of the South-West by Lord Astor and herself, he observed the conventions by arriving in a very smart dark suit, but his irrepressible humour ran away with him in his speech. 'Many of you may think,' he said, 'I am an enthusiastic advocate of university education, whereas I am fully convinced that the English university is destroying civilisation and has, for some centuries, been making

(Above) The dining room at 'Shaw's Corner', the room in which he died. On the right-hand wall is a portrait of him by Augustus John.
(Right) Alice Laden, Shaw's housekeeper, in the garden at 'Shaw's Corner', 1946.

(Right) **GBS** and two-year-old Michael who asked him if he was the liftman *(see* p 165*)* and *(below)* cameras poised at Shaw's garden-party at Malvern, August 1932 *(Radio Times Hulton Picture Library)*.

decent government and decent life for the people impossible.... The thing to do to these venerable institutions, particularly Oxford and Cambridge, in spite of the beauty of many of their buildings, is to raze them to the ground and sow the foundations with salt. If it is too much trouble to knock them down, use them as asylums for lunatics.'

Despite their close friendship and her constant visits to Shaw's Corner, Lady Astor was not, Mrs Laden says, always a welcome visitor. 'I remember she phoned on his ninetieth birthday to say that she would be coming to see him. "Tell her I would rather she didn't come." A little later that morning a telegram arrived from her saying: "My present to you is my absence." '

Pandit Jawaharlal Nehru, India's first Prime Minister, while in England for the Conference of Commonwealth Prime Ministers in 1949, travelled by car all the way to Ayot St Lawrence in between his other engagements, and they sat together in the dining-room talking for nearly two hours; then the visitor was taken for a walk round the garden because he loved flowers and he expressed his surprise that there were none in the vases in the house. He was told what Shaw said many times to his visitors: 'I love children, but I don't cut off their heads and stick them in vases all over the place.' Nehru had brought him a basket of mangoes all the way from India by air. He handed it to Mrs Laden and explained how they should be cut up and served; mangoes were not normally obtainable in England at that time. 'Let him have one for breakfast tomorrow,' Nehru said. When Shaw came to the table the next morning he glared at the fruit, then rang the bell. Mrs Laden, realising it must be the mango, signalled to Maggie to go in. The bell was rung again. On entering, Maggie saw him holding out the plate of luscious pink mango so carefully and painstakingly prepared. 'Here,' cried Shaw, 'take this to Mrs Laden and tell her to throw it into the dustbin.'

Sir Robert Ho Tung, the very wealthy Chinese industrialist who had met Shaw in Hong Kong, was another welcome visitor. 'He was a strikingly picturesque figure and a very old man – it is not easy to guess the age of the Chinese people. He brought with him a nurse and a private detective, a secretary and an interpreter; they filled the small dining-room. He handed Mr Shaw a very beautiful blue Chinese robe and gave me a lovely black chiffon dress with a large red mandarin button. Sir Robert talked to Mr Shaw about Hong Kong and supplied details for the Chinese scene in *Buoyant Billions*, which Mr Shaw was then writing.

'After they had gone we discovered that Sir Robert had left his spectacles behind. We asked the chauffeur to take them in the Rolls to his suite in the Dorchester Hotel. He was so delighted that he sent me a box of embroidered Chinese handkerchiefs. Mr Shaw asked me what I thought of Sir Robert. I said: "He must be a hundred years old." Mr Shaw laughed. "He isn't," he said. "He is a chicken compared to me. He is only eighty-two. The difference is that he has twenty wives and I have none – now." I said: "I don't know why he brought such a large escort." He spoke English quite well. I couldn't see the need for the interpreter unless it was to help out the others. Anyway with five of them there, not one seemed to have remembered his glasses.'

Bertrand Russell did not come very often. Mrs Laden remembers in particular one visit when Shaw and he were closeted together in the dining-room and she heard loud, angry voices coming from inside. 'I have never known Mr Shaw to lose to his temper. He had astonishing self-control. It must have been Mr Russell who was angry and Mr Shaw raised his voice only to be heard. There certainly was a heated argument of some sort going on. After about two hours they both came out and Mr Shaw saw Bertrand Russell to the door in silence. Not a word was said by either of them. They didn't shake hands, nor did they say goodbye. After Mr Russell had gone Mr Shaw turned and I noticed that his face was red. It was the only time I saw any hint of anger in his countenance in all the years I was with him.'

Well-known actresses often came to see him. Vivien Leigh, who played the lead in *The Doctor's Dilemma* on the stage in London and in the film version of *Caesar and Cleopatra*, told me of the advice he had given her about her rôles: he was ninety when she played Cleopatra. Personally, she said, she did not know him well, though he made a fuss of her when she went to see him at Ayot. 'He liked her enormously,' says Mrs Laden. 'They used to walk in the garden together arm in arm.'

Greer Garson, who had appeared in his play *Too True to be Good*, in which the character of Private Meek ('dusty and gritty, but very alert') was based on T E Lawrence, was another welcome visitor.

'I was filming at MGM's studios near London,' Greer told me, 'and often visited Shaw's Corner at weekends. Sometimes he greeted me in the garden, leaning on a heavy cane. He, who had been a tireless hiker and climber, exhausting all younger companions, complained indignantly: "I'm having a bit of trouble with me legs." He wanted me to play in his latest comedy – then on a pre-London tryout. "Not on your life," sez I, very bold. "That's a part for a blonde and you already have a beautiful, clever leading lady in it. Now why don't you write me a part for a redhead?" "I'll do that next season," he promised. ". . . you ought to do *Captain Brassbound's Conversion* – it was rather special because I wrote it for Ellen Terry and you are Ellen Terry's natural successor." From him this was a rare compliment and I was aglow.

'I thought he liked to be visited, although he complained once to me that people were always coming to see him and insisting on introducing their little children. "Their idea, I suppose, is to be able to tell their children when they're grown up: just think, you were patted on the head by George Bernard Shaw! And of course the children are going to say: Who the hell is Bernard Shaw?"

'On another occasion when GBS escorted me to the car after tea I introduced him to my pretty aunt from Scotland and her friend, a charming, vivacious Polish countess. They had been for a drive to look at the pleasant countryside. "Times have certainly changed," he commented. "Once the mothers and aunts used to come to see me and sent the young girls away to wait elsewhere so they wouldn't, presumably, be exposed to my dangerous influence. Now the young ladies come to visit me and send their attractive aunts away!" '

'Greer Garson's visits were always a great joy to Mr Shaw,' Mrs Laden told me. 'She was a gay, infectious personality and whenever she was in London she phoned or wrote to ask if she could come, and his answer was always eagerly in the affirmative. On one occasion she sent me a delightful letter. "Dear Mrs Laden", she wrote from the Dorchester Hotel on the 19th September 1949, "I had the pleasure on my recent crossing from New York, of bringing with me a parcel of Ivory Soap (it floats!) for Mr Shaw, and some nylons for yourself which Mr Gabriel Pascal asked me to bring over. I didn't write to you immediately on my arrival as I was plunged into a whirl of preparations for the film we are making over here (sequel to *Mrs Miniver*)". When she came Greer produced a mouth organ and played music-hall ditties which Mr Shaw sang most lustily.

'On one occasion she motored to Ayot through a dense fog and arrived hours late. I was giving a Christmas Eve party for the two maids, who had invited their friends from the village, and Mr Shaw and Greer both came up to our part of the house and went into the bedroom on the first floor where drinks were being served. I shall always remember him with a lump of cake in his hand as he talked to the Rector, Mr Davies, and his wife and our other guests. He did not stay very long. "Dear! Dear! Dear!" he exclaimed, "what an extraordinary party," and left.'

Another actress, Ellen Pollock, now President of the Shaw Society, had known him for a number of years. She first met him with some trepidation at Malvern where, as a very young actress, she was selected to play the leading rôle of Sweetie in his new play *Too True to be Good*, which was given its first performance in England at the Festival there on the 6th August 1932. Married to the artist, James Proudfoot, she had with her their two-year-old son Michael. Seeing Shaw descend in the hotel lift, for which they had been waiting, the child mistook the great man for the lift boy and told him to which floor to take them. Ellen chided him, but Shaw checked her. 'Leave him alone,' he said. 'He shows plenty of individuality.' He stayed in the lift and took them up to their floor. The next morning, on ringing for the lift, the boy asked, 'Where's the lift boy?'

There was a two-week option on Ellen Pollock's services for the London production of the play. Doubts as to whether she would be retained caused her the utmost anxiety. Shaw's wife came to the rescue. 'Don't worry, Ellen,' she said. 'You will be playing in the West End. GBS is resolved on that.' Ellen told me: 'I can't tell you how relieved I was to hear that and to find myself in that important rôle when the play opened at the New Theatre in London. I was very lucky, for I was completely unknown. In the cast with me were such great actors as Cedric Hardwicke, Ralph Richardson and, later, Donald Wolfit, all three of them knights. GBS was kind enough, later, to introduce me to T E Lawrence, on whom the character of Meek in that play was based.

'I had a snapshot of my son Michael with GBS, which I stuck into the mirror of my dressing-table at the theatre. A newspaper reporter, seeing it, asked if he could reproduce it in his paper. I said, "I must ask Mr Shaw's permission." His reply was: "Bless you, my child, of course I don't mind. But if the public infer that I am the parent of the child, please don't blame me." '

Ellen Pollock often visited him at Ayot, accompanied

sometimes by her son Michael, by then a schoolboy. A warm affection grew up between the boy and the man he had once called 'the lift-boy'. Ellen says: 'As you know, GBS hated having his birthday remembered or receiving any gifts to mark the occasion – and Christmas presents too were taboo. I discovered this quite early. After giving him one or two to mark the occasion, I was told quite sternly: "You and I are artists, Ellen. If you continue to do this our ways will part." So I stopped. But I could not resist giving him an expanding book-rest, though I took care not to send it to him for either his birthday or for Christmas. He accepted it and sent me this delightful note: "The book-rest expands in my study and your love in my wintry old heart" – with a rough drawing to represent the heart.'

Wendy Hiller also came to see him. She sent him a small gift two years before he died and he thanked her for it in rhyme: the blue postcard, dated the 6th February 1948, states:

> '*Postman knocks*
> *Gloves and socks*
> *From Miss Hiller*
> *What a thriller!*'

During the war, when it was not easy to get transport from Beaconsfield where she lives, she and her husband Ronald Gow covered the twenty-five miles across country to Ayot on bicycles. 'We couldn't cycle there and back on the same day,' says Wendy, 'so what we did was to stay for a night or two in a very pleasant and comfortable inn at Codicote, which is about a mile or so from Ayot; and we went to see GBS the next day. We had some delightful hours with him, spent another night at the nearby inn and then cycled back home. GBS was very pleased to see us, and our talk ranged over the years – from the Malvern Festival when I first met him, to the two films of his in which I appeared. We talked hardly at all about the war. He was nearly ninety at the time. but in no way infirm, still tall, slim, very upright, bright-eyed and clear-headed, and, as always, most amusing.'

Mrs Laden adds: 'But I think Mr Shaw enjoyed most the visits of Gaby Pascal. One never knew when he was coming. He would phone to say he was on his way, but at times he didn't even do that but just arrived. And he always came laden with the most wonderful gifts – cakes, biscuits, chocolates, candies and other things he had brought back from America. Mr Shaw, though he rebuked him for his extravagance, knowing that Gaby was always hard up, was as delighted as a child, opening the boxes, nibbling the chocolates. Then they would sit down and talk, mostly about future films, and Gaby would tell him where he had been and what he had done. And when it was time for Gaby to leave, he would always go up to Mr Shaw, take his hand and with a gentle smile say: "I seem to have run out of money. Is it possible for you to lend me some?" Mr Shaw always responded. It seemed to me that in the end Mr Shaw really paid for the gifts Gaby had brought him. I liked Gaby. He was a strange character, round face, a bushy head of hair, greying slightly, a charming foreign accent, and so very kind and considerate; he never failed to bring something for me too. We got on extremely well, so much so that Mr Shaw commented on it once. He said: "You won't allow me to come into your kitchen. I have to talk to you through the serving hatch. And when Lady Astor went in one day you promptly ordered her out. Yet Gabriel is always welcome. You two sit there and have coffee together and laugh and talk." I said: "Mr Shaw, the kitchen is to me what your dining-room and your hut in the garden are to you. It's where I work and where occasionally I entertain. Mr Pascal looks on me as a friend and if he wants to have a cup of coffee with me, naturally I invite him to join me there."

'Sometimes Mr Shaw could be most trying. At the last minute, without any prior warning, he would expect me to wave a wand and produce something he wanted. I was on my way out for the afternoon when Maggie came after me and said: "Can you prepare tea for three people this afternoon?" I was flabbergasted. "Where does he think I can get tea from? Doesn't he realise that with rationing still on, we are finding it extremely difficult to manage? Explain that to him," I said. When I returned in the evening Maggie told me that Mr Shaw had been asking for me and was waiting to see me. As I approached the dining-room door I heard him say to Maggie, who had preceded me: "Never mind. Don't send her in." But I was already there, so I opened the door and went in. He was standing by the fire. "You sent for me?" I asked. "You let me down very badly today," he said. "I've never let you down," I replied. He then explained that three people had come for tea. "You should have told me earlier," I said. "Who were they?" "I don't know them," he said. "They wanted to see me and I thought I'd give them some tea." "Mr Shaw, you don't have any tea – ever. I use your ration of tea for the staff. That makes it barely enough for them and there's nothing over for visitors, let alone for people you don't even know. You really must think about this before you ask people to tea." I then left. He could see I was cross. The next morning he sent for me and said: "Never mind about yesterday," and then, I being Scottish, he began to sing Harry Lauder's song "I love a Lassie". He always had a pleasant way of smoothing things over.'

Other visitors at Ayot were Ingrid Bergman, whom Pascal brought along for a part in the film *Caesar and Cleopatra*, but she was not free; Lilli Palmer and her then husband Rex Harrison; Edith Evans; Isobel Jeans; Gene Tunney, the former heavyweight champion of the world; and Danny Kaye. When Danny wrote to ask if he could come, Shaw replied on one of his pale blue postcards: 'Keep off. You are a young man, what do you want to see an old man for?' But he came nevertheless. 'He arrived after lunch,' says Mrs Laden, 'and Mr Shaw was having his afternoon sleep in the dining-room. Mr Kaye walked in the garden for a while and saw Mr Shaw at about 4.30. But unfortunately Danny Kaye had to rush back to the Palladium where he was appearing. He cut his departure so fine that when he left in his car, his chauffeur crashed into Mr Harding's car outside the local pub, The Brocket Arms. The damage fortunately was not serious and Danny Kaye was able to get to the Palladium in time.'

Alfred Hitchcock, the rotund film director famous for his thrillers, called one day and after the preliminary handshakes said affably: 'One look at you, Mr Shaw, and I know there's famine in the land,' to which Shaw replied: 'One look at you, Mr Hitchcock, and I know who caused it.'

One day a woman they didn't know arrived wearing a black house-coat. 'She was about forty years old and had long red fingernails. I asked her what she wanted. She wouldn't say, but insisted on seeing Mr Shaw. I told her that unless he knew what it was about he wouldn't see her. She was a very determined woman. Nothing would induce her to leave. She went into the garden and lay on the grass, clawing the earth. Mr Shaw saw her through the window and asked me who she was. I explained that she refused to say anything except to him. He watched her for a moment and then said: "I'll see her." I took her in. She was with Mr Shaw for half an hour. What they talked about he didn't say. That was unlike him, for he always had something to say about the strangers who pestered him. It was obviously something personal and private concerning the woman, and Mr Shaw felt he shouldn't discuss it. He was not the sort of person who would prevaricate. I found him to be a very truthful man – he wouldn't even tell a white lie.'

15
Shaw as a Villager

THOUGH AT FIRST Shaw did not much care for the village of Ayot St Lawrence, he grew in time to love it. Almost every evening he set out with his hat and stick and camera to wander through its few familiar streets and stop to talk to people: he had got to know most of them.

'All in all they liked him and were proud that so great a man was living in their midst,' Mrs Laden told me. 'A few thought he was a snob – I cannot understand why because he certainly wasn't that; others, mostly those living in the large houses and with strong Conservative convictions, didn't want to know him because he was a Socialist and possibly even a Communist – he had said he was often enough; and there were those who remembered his anti-war views and regarded him as a traitor. But, happily, there were exceptions, even among them.

'The rector, the Rev R J Davies, liked him enormously. He was a relatively young man, about forty, I would say, very kind and extremely good company.'

Canon Davies, as he is now, told me that Mr Shaw knew that some people in the village criticised him, but he dismissed them, saying that was because they did not really know him. Those who knew him found that he was a wonderful person. To him we were all fellow human beings.

'He was very interested in the church. He wrote to me once to tell me that the façade of our Palladian church was at one time obscured and spoilt by four trees. "I got them cut down," Mr Shaw said in his letter, "by offering to pay the woodman. But he left one which

170

was then just a shrub, but now is a horrible disfigurement and makes an attractive photo of the façade impossible." He also subscribed towards the restoration of the church.'

Unfailingly Shaw's daily visit was to the post office, sometimes to buy stamps, but generally just for a chat with the widowed postmistress, Mrs Jisbella Lyth, in her half-timbered, five-centuries-old cottage. Shaw used to spend most of the week in London at first, but wherever he was he used to write to her to send him the stamps he needed, and always enclosed a cheque; often the cheque was for £5 worth of stamps. She told him it was so easy for him to get them in London and at Ayot a maid could have come across from the house for them, but he always wrote a note in his own hand for the stamps. 'My good woman,' he replied, 'you should be pleased. You will be able to sell my letters for half a crown a time when I am dead.' She smiled at this and told him: 'I sell them for ten shillings and sixpence each now.' He was astonished. 'We'll have to go halves on that,' he said. Among the postcards she used to sell at the post office, which was also a general store, were a photograph of Mr Shaw (taken by the famous Canadian photographer Karsh) and one of his house, Shaw's Corner.

Mrs Laden told me: 'His going to see Mrs Lyth so regularly was the talk of the village. People used to say that he was in love with her and, being a widower, was possibly thinking of marrying her. But in fact he was only amusing himself and did not care a jot what anyone said.'

Mrs Lyth was said to have inspired the character of the woman in Shaw's short play *A Village Wooing*, which he wrote during the winter of 1932–3 while on a voyage round the world in the *Empress of Britain*. Mrs Lyth's own comment was 'I don't know when he ever saw me wooing anybody'. The part, which was of a middle-aged woman who ran a village shop and post office, was played on the stage in London by Sybil Thorndike; Arthur Wontner played the man, a bearded writer. Wontner's wife and children called at the post office one afternoon to see Mrs Lyth and suggested that she should go and see the play. 'I did. It was a curtain-raiser for Galsworthy's play *The Little Man*, which I actually preferred. I got a lot of publicity from Mr Shaw's play and it was as a result of it that he discovered that my real name was Jisbella and not Jessie.'

'Not all the top people in the village,' says Mrs Laden, 'refused to know Mr Shaw. Captain and Mrs Lionel Ames and his mother, for example, were very good friends of his. They lived quite close to Shaw's Corner. The Captain, a great landowner, who once owned Mr Shaw's house, knew him longer than anyone else in the village, in fact ever since the Shaws moved into Ayot in 1906. He told me: "Mr Shaw was one of the most amiable persons I have ever met. He talked a lot of nonsense about being a Socialist. He wasn't a Socialist at all, but a Conservative, in my opinion."

'Just before Mr Shaw died we had a bonfire in the garden and the smoke, I was sorry to see, blew into Captain Ames's garden. I had a phone call about it and Mr Shaw instantly sent a letter of apology to the Captain. It was one of the last letters he wrote. "Dear Lionel Ames," he said, "I thought of you very sympathetically on Saturday when the west wind was smoking you out. You will have your revenge when the wind goes south and smokes me out. I know of no remedy for the autumn bonfires, which have smoked for all my 94 years and thousands of centuries before that. . . . I shall be burnt up myself presently; but the fumes will get no further than Golders Green. Your phone-call to Mrs Laden reached her in a moment when a terrible misfortune had just overtaken her. Our pet cat had died in the night; and she was overwhelmed with grief. Forgive her if she vented any of it on you – GBS." The cat was mine and I was shattered, but Mr Shaw was fond of her too. That was possibly the last letter he wrote. He died four weeks later.'

Then there was Carola Oman, the historian, who was married to Sir Gerald Lenanton. They were near neighbours and lived in the seventeenth-century Bride Hall on the Wheathampstead Road. 'I saw him often,' Lady Lenanton states, 'and never came away without a gift of a book from him. He inscribed several to me. What a marvellous actor he would have made. He had a beautiful voice. He could imitate Henry Irving particularly well, especially as the Jew in *The Bells*, and he was wonderful as Macbeth.'

There were others. Mr and Mrs Harold Thompson lived in an attractive Tudor cottage by the post office and their two young daughters, Audrey and Rosemary, used to come, their plaits hanging down their backs, to sit with Mrs Laden in the kitchen. Mrs Thompson told me that she often saw Shaw walking through the village with his camera. 'He sometimes stopped to talk, mostly he was friendly, but occasionally he was quite abrupt. He asked me if he could photograph my son Clive, who was eighteen months old at the time. I held the child up in my arms for the picture and Mr Shaw sent me two copies of it. Another time he photographed Clive riding a broomstick.

'Following a fall in London Mr Shaw was walking through the village leaning heavily on two sticks and greeted me as I wheeled my little boy in a pram. "I wish," he said, "you would put me in the pram and take *me* back to my home."

'He took an interest in village affairs and especially in the church. He used to gaze at the pretty old church from across the park and talked to the warden again and again about cutting down one tree in the churchyard which obscured his view. But it wasn't done, unfortunately. Quite often he sent things for the sale-of-work to help the church funds and I know he sent an annual sum to the rector for the church as pew rent.'

Mrs Thompson's younger daughter Rosemary (now Mrs Horton) told me: 'He was very kind to us when we

173

were children. Even when he saw us in the distance he would raise his stick and wave it. He autographed one of his books for each of us. One day, seeing my sister returning from school, he asked her what she was studying and when she told him Shakespeare, he said: "I shall never allow any of my books to be used for school lessons. It isn't fair to inflict them on the children. I don't want them to grow up and loathe me." '

His interest in the village's activities led him to help in little ways that reveal his thoughtfulness. He used to take a sheet music of madrigals round for the choir to try, and supplied a list of his gramophone records which he offered to lend if needed; they included Elgar's works, Mozart's operas and Irish folk-songs. He even responded, after some persuasion, to an appeal to address the local Women's Institute, and two years before his death he 'unveiled' a new wrought-iron gate for which the residents had subscribed for the old ruined abbey.

Shaw was sensitive about the village's attitude towards him. 'Those who don't know me have the worst thoughts about me,' he said.

16
Vanity

THE VANITY so often evident in Shaw had its roots, one feels, in the early years which saw the creation of his public image to lift him from the inferiority he felt as a child and as a schoolboy. Even when, with the coming of world acclaim and recognition as a genius, the public image was no longer needed and was used merely through long habit and with a jesting braggadocio, the vanity remained.

He never passed a mirror either in his home or in public places without turning to glance at himself in it. The beard, grown when he was twenty-five to hide, he says, the slight scars of smallpox (actually he had arrived in London five years earlier with a scanty beard that looked as if a goat had nibbled it) – the beard became in time a symbol of recognition, and he liked recognition, though he often complained that he was pursued by crowds for his autograph. He found it impossible to walk as other normal human beings could through the streets, or to visit a theatre and cinema, or to dine in a hotel. H G Wells suggested a solution. 'The remedy is in your own hands,' he said. 'Just shave off your beard.' To this Shaw gave no answer, and the beard was retained until the end of his life.

Mrs Laden says: 'He gave a great deal of attention to his appearance. He not only had hair-do's but beard-do's and eyebrow-do's as well with rigid regularity from the barber at Welwyn; he also had his head and face massaged and his nails manicured on these occasions.' While living in London Shaw had his beard and hair shampooed by the Ogilvie Sisters in their fashionable coiffeur establishment; and during his trip to Russia he got Lady Astor to wash his beard.

'He was very particular about his clothes, too,' Mrs Laden added. 'Although he dressed unconventionally in knickerbockers and a Norfolk jacket, he had a vast wardrobe filled with long-trousered dark suits, which he wore sometimes, and a great range and variety of Norfolk jackets and knee-breeches. These were specially made for him by his tailor in Savile Row; they cost a lot of money. And his cupboards were choked with neckties, all of which were also specially designed and made for him.

'Then there were his hats. . . so many of them that it is impossible to count them. A great many were just caps, mostly in checks with different combinations of colour. Quite a number of Homburgs were in the collection – black, grey and brown, and so on. He also had some sombreros, large ten-gallon hats, one of them a fawn one with a band of many colours. His favourite was his oldest sombrero in which he was photographed in 1891. He said it needed repair and sprucing up and asked it I could get it done. Fortunately I was able to deal with it and he was so pleased that he gave me the old photograph of him wearing the hat. On the back he wrote: "To Alice Laden at Ayot St Lawrence in my 94th year – G Bernard Shaw. When this old hat was new, so was I."

'He loved old things and would not part with any of them. Even after he was ninety he kept ordering new clothes, some only a year or two before his death, and he clung to the old, torn, shabby garments for garden wear. He had very sharp bones and his knees worked their way through his trousers. I used to mend them and put patches underneath. His shoes were mostly of the brogue type, with long leather tongues falling over the laces; they too were numerous, mostly in black or tan. He always wore mittens, often indoors as well as out. If it was raining he put on his black wool mittens and selected an umbrella from the abundant display of them in the

Shaw speaking at a protest meeting against a visit from the Czar, about 1910 (*Radio Times Hulton Picture Library*). GBS at work *(below)* in the seclusion of his hut in the garden of his Ayot St Lawrence home *(Keystone)*.

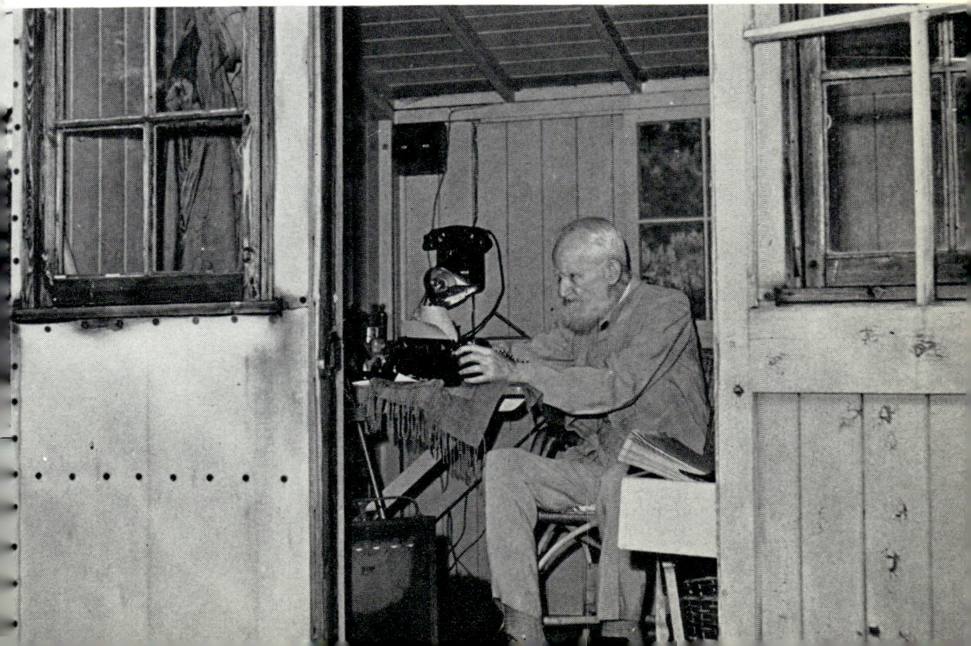

(Left) 1949 – informal rehearsals of *Buoyant Billions*, with Denholm Elliott, Mrs Winsten, wife of one of Shaw's neighbours, and Frances Day *(Radio Times Hulton Picture Library)*. (Below) Shaw with Rex Harrison and Robert Morley on the set of the film *Major Barbara*.

hall; but when he was better dressed his mittens were of fawn-coloured lambs' wool.'

The outer trappings were not his only concern. His figure had to be right too and so he did physical jerks daily. 'He was able to touch his toes until he was over ninety and after completing the conventional exercises in the house he used to go down to his hut at the end of the garden and lock the door for a while, unlocking it only when he settled down to work. I used to wonder what he was up to, so I peeped through the window and saw the old man down on his knees, bending backwards until his head touched the ground. Many men half his age would not have been able to do that. His arms were very strong and he had a very powerful grip when he shook hands, as you know.

'He watched his weight all the time. He weighed himself every day and if he found he was as little as an ounce up, I was told to cut down on the meals. Every ingredient of every dish of his food was weighed: this had quite as much to do with his care of his health as with his vanity about his figure. He was resolved on keeping it to the end. His mind was vigorous right up to his death, though his memory was a little shaky in the last year or two. His walk remained as brisk as ever and I used often to see him come bouncing down the stairs even after he was ninety – at times he even danced down the stairs.

'One cannot get away from the fact that he was vain. He needed glasses, but wouldn't wear them and consequently he often passed people in the street without recognising them. Whenever he expected guests he went to a mirror to see that he looked all right. He knew he was handsome and he was very proud of that. He used to flirt with almost every woman who came to the house, except Lady Astor and even she got playfully chaffed. It was, of course, quite harmless; he enjoyed it and so did they, I think. Most of the women who came were young and pretty.'

An amusing thing happened one day and Mrs Laden chortled as she told me of it. 'Maggie crept softly down the stairs and tiptoed into the kitchen. Her face was flushed. "What do you think," she said. "Mr Shaw is in the passage upstairs trying on one of your frocks." I knew he was fond of nice clothes. But why my frock? I couldn't believe it. I hurried up the stairs. The door of his bedroom was slightly ajar and I could see him reflected in the mirror, wearing one of my dresses. I went in. He turned and smiled at me. 'What do you think you are doing?" I asked. "This Chinese robe Sir Robert Ho Tung gave me is most attractive. I thought I'd try it on." "That's my dress," I said. "Sir Robert gave you a blue robe – this one is black." I knew he was a little colour-blind. He couldn't distinguish blue from green as a rule, though he did get the colour of his wife's eyes right; they certainly were green. But black and blue!

'The confusion arose because my clothes cupboard stood in the passage between his section of the house and ours, and he had an overflow cupboard there for the clothes he no longer wore. I brought out the Chinese robe for him and he was later photographed in it.' Shaw gave a postcard size print of this to Sybil Thorndike, who has used it ever since as a bookmarker in her Bible.

Further evidence of his vanity was provided by the Press photographers; Shaw could never resist posing before a camera. His wife, on the other hand, was camera-shy, she would turn away, and avoided publicity so persistently that many people who knew of Shaw and had seen his plays were unaware that he was married. In his study at the foot of the stairs at Ayot he had a row of caricatures of himself done by well-known artists. His drawing-room was full of busts. One of them was by Rodin; Charlotte had had that done and paid for it, for Rodin had never heard of Shaw and, when approached, tried to avoid accepting the commission, 'but my wife,'

Shaw tells us, 'would not be put off.' She enquired of his secretary what the charge would be and was told that Rodin was paid £1,000 for a marble bust and £800 for one in bronze. Charlotte promptly sent him a cheque for £1,000 – ' as a contribution,' she said, 'not a commission,' and added that there was no obligation for him to make the bust or, if he began work on it, to finish it. Rodin invited Shaw to Paris and the very next morning the Shaws with feverish haste were in his studio. That was in April 1906, when Shaw was forty-nine. After a month of sittings, when the bust was nearly finished, Rodin stopped work and said he could carry it no further, but would go on with it whenever Shaw happened to be in Paris. It was never completed. 'Rodin,' says Shaw, 'with his callipers was extremely conscientious in getting the visible facts right. . . . I am a civilised Irishman with a thin skin and hair of exceptionally fine texture, always well brushed. Though six-foot high, I weighed only ten stone instead of twelve stone or thereabouts. I am a brain worker, not a manual worker. All this Rodin conveyed perfectly. . . . He gave that in the bust unmistakably. But I am a comedian as well as a philosopher; and Rodin had no sense of humour. I think I saw him laugh once, when I took a specially sweet tit-bit from Madame Rodin and gave half of it to his dog Kap. I am not quite sure that he went so far as to laugh even then. Accordingly, the bust has no sense of humour; and Shaw without a sense of humour is not quite Shaw.' The language barrier was a serious handicap, for Shaw was unable to ask his way in any language other than English. Rodin said of the bust, '*C'est une vrai tête de Christ.*' That was the first bust ever done of Shaw and it (or a copy of it) was one of seven in the drawing-room at Ayot St Lawrence.

Shaw sat next for Prince Paul Troubetskoy, who said of Rodin's work, 'This face has no eyes. All Rodin's busts are blind.' Others followed. The last sculptor to do a head of Shaw was Jacob Epstein, who told me when I was in his studio a very few days after Shaw's death that Charlotte disliked it and would not have the bust in the house. Epstein brought it out from behind the massive Christs on which he had been working and I thought it was a remarkably fine likeness of Shaw. 'He wrote me a long letter about it,' Epstein told me. 'In it he said that each of the sculptors who had attempted to portray him in marble or bronze made him in their own likeness. "Rodin made me look like a French bourgeois, which I am not. Troubetskoy, being a Russian prince, made me look like a member of the effete Russian aristocracy." And so on, coming finally to me. "You, Jacob Epstein," he wrote, "also made me in your own image. I became a Brooklyn navvy in your hands. My wife saw it and said that if that bust came into our house she would walk out. I may possess only a veneer over what you seem to see as a Brooklyn navvy, but without that veneer I am not Bernard Shaw, and without the lift at the outer ends of my eyebrows I am just a barbarous joker and not a comedian. Your bust is a masterpiece, but it is not a portrait of me." I have the letter somewhere but that is the gist of it.'

Dame Laura Knight met Shaw for the first time at a tea-party at Malvern during one of the summer Festivals. 'When we were introduced,' Laura Knight told me, 'he gave me an indifferent handshake and walked away, but after a few minutes he returned and shook my hand more warmly. "I hear you are *Laura* Knight," he said. "I was told Mrs Knight. You might have been any Mrs Knight." One Sunday evening he came to talk to Barry Jackson's guests at the Lawnside School. I suddenly felt a dig in my back and turning saw that it was Shaw. He said: "I am offended with you. You've never asked me to pose for you." I smiled and said: "Well, I'll ask you now." I began work on the picture in the school hall. At the same time a Hungarian sculptor named Strobl was busy modelling a bust of him. This made it extremely difficult for me because a sculptor views the sitter from various angles and so moves him about whereas a painter wants him to sit still and present the same facial angle all the time. The position is fixed and cannot be altered. So I was obviously at a great disadvantage with the sculptor there. Shaw's chair was perched rather precariously on a small packing-case. The sculptor wanted me to make Shaw talk. I tried but in fact GBS did all the talking. He said: "Have you noticed the projection at the back of my skull? It is supposed to mean excessive sexual development. Catherine of Russia had the same. And my ears – they are very big. Have you noticed that? When I was a child, my nurse used to cling on to my petticoats for fear my ears might act as sails and carry me away."

'While GBS was being moved about by the sculptor I did a number of drawings from various angles to fill in time. The portrait itself was held up until the sculptor finished his work and finally left. I then had him to myself. While I worked he sang through the complete score of many operas, one after the other. When I finished, Shaw noticed that the panelled walls and the parquet floor of the hall were splashed with the sculptor's plaster. "Who's going to clean up this dreadful mess?" he asked me. I told him that I had already arranged for two charladies to come and do the work. Shaw insisted on paying. We argued. The sculptor, I said, had already given me half a crown for the cleaners. "Keep that to pay for your taxi when you take your materials back to your hotel." But he sent me home in his car and I gave the Hungarian sculptor's half a crown and my own as a tip to the chauffeur.

'The greatest weakness I detected in Shaw was for the Press photographers. He admitted this: "If I hear the click of a camera, I stand up straight at once and look my best." He always carried a camera himself and took two snapshots of me, but the results, I'm afraid, were rather misty.'

In the summer of 1936 on his eightieth birthday Shaw

was asked to plant a mulberry tree in the public gardens in Malvern. 'He showed off magnificently before the large assembled crowd,' says Laura Knight. 'First he peeled off his Norfolk jacket with its strap down the back and a belt at the waist, folded it carefully while we watched, and laid it very neatly on the ground. Then he rolled up his shirt sleeves, spat on his hands and picked up the spade. The soil had already been loosened for him, but GBS dug deep into it with tremendous force as though breaking the resisting surface with his immense strength, then with a repeated rhythmic gesture he drew up great clods of earth and tossed them away. There was a lightning display of flashbulbs and when at last the performance was over there was a thunder of applause.'

The mulberry tree planted, there was dancing round it – 'led by GBS and Elspeth,' Stewart Granger told me; both Granger and Elspeth March (his wife at the time) were appearing in Shaw's plays in the Festival.

Laura Knight smilingly added: 'A day or two after planting the mulberry, Shaw, Charlotte and I were on the terrace of Mount Pleasant Hotel. Near us was a large mulberry tree with its luscious berries strewn about the turf. Shaw stared at them unbelievingly. "Blackberries do not grow on trees," he said, "or do they?" '

'He could be very blunt and rude. He once told me: "I've never heard such damned nonsense as you talk." But if alone with you he could also be most modest. He acknowledged that he knew nothing about painting since Burne-Jones. Though he always appeared to be very certain about his own work, he confessed that he was often dissatisfied and went on revising until he got it right.'

Shaw told Feliks Topolski, who did a series of brilliant drawings of him: 'Your pictures make me look years too old. I won't look like that even when your recently born child comes of age.'

182

H G Wells described Shaw's vanity as his most estranging fault. 'Shaw was fantastically vain. He was ruled by a naked, unqualified, ego-centred, devouring vanity such as one rarely meets in life.

17
His Death

THAT SHAW HAD a strong constitution is obvious; to it he owed his longevity, as also of course to his careful and constant attention to his health. His desire to be long-lived was indicated when he was only half-way through his allotted span. Early in his temporary stay at Ayot St Lawrence, while wandering through the churchyard, he stopped to read an inscription on a tombstone, which said: 'Jane Eversley. Born 1815. Died 1895.' Below were inscribed these words: 'Her time was short.' Shaw scratched at the right side of his beard reflectively and turning to his wife he said: 'This is the place for me,' and there he remained until his death in his ninety-fifth year.

He had various ailments, the worst of which were his migraines, which afflicted him with regularity once a month. The headaches were so blinding that he generally locked himself in his room and would not allow even his wife to come in: treatment of various kinds was tried but without avail. He had smallpox before the age of twenty-five and recurrent bouts of influenza. During his many travels he was always seasick – 'holidays always leave me a wreck' – and at times, despite his care with his diet, he had colic and other stomach upsets. But he had to take to his bed far more frequently because of various mishaps, most of them caused by his own folly. Cycling and motoring accidents kept recurring; and his imprudence over a swollen ankle led to his getting married on crutches.

'He never spoke about his health: it was really astonishingly robust,' says Mrs Laden. 'He had the stomach of an ox and could digest anything. I used to wonder at first at the vast quantities of raw vegetables he ate – our insides aren't strong enough for that and a great many people would certainly have suffered from acute indigestion after eating some of his food; but his inside had become attuned to it and he never had any discomfort. He used to boast that he was ten times as fit as any meat-eater. "But vegetarians need more exercise, a sedentary life is all right for the carnivorous. Animals that live on grass and leaves are the most ferocious and so are vegetarians." He really believed all that, but I have never met a more self-controlled man – there was nothing ferocious about him. He may have seemed excitable because he came out with all sorts of fantastic statements that no one could agree with and he gesticulated a lot when he talked and quite often he used the word "bloody", which caused such a sensation when Mrs Patrick Campbell used it on the stage in *Pygmalion*. But I've never seen him in a temper.

'Mind you, quite a lot of things irritated him. He disliked noise. There had to be no noise of any sort in the house when he was indoors. We weren't allowed to use the Hoover until he went to the hut. There were two separate staircases and the staff used the one that was away from his, but even so we could not laugh or talk in raised voices on the stairs or in the kitchen, nor were we allowed to have a radio in the kitchen; it was all right in our own rooms with the doors between the two sections of the house firmly shut. Dripping taps was another thing he could not stand. "Do something about it," he would say. "I can't stand it another minute." If there was any noise in the street outside, all the windows of his room had to be shut at once. As a rule his wife and he, when they were alone, never talked during meals. He wanted silence and she observed it. When later she began to depart from this rule he put the radio on softly while they ate.

'When he criticised any of the staff and we answered

back, as some would call it, he didn't give a rap. That sort of thing never worried him. He allowed you to make your point. But what he didn't like was being put in the wrong – that seemed to annoy him and he clung to his original opinion, as so many of his greatest critics discovered through the years. Nothing seemed to ruffle him really: if it could be controlled it was dealt with at once, if it couldn't be controlled, he just put up with it. I remember the day a bomb fell into the garden of the house next door. All the windows at Shaw's Corner were blown out. I rushed into the dining-room to see if he was all right and found him standing in the middle of the room quite unperturbed.'

A few months before his death Shaw wrote a long letter to Ivor Brown, the author and dramatic critic, explaining why he had uttered disparaging comments about Shakespeare and his work: he once said he wanted to dig Shakespeare out of his grave and throw stones at him. Writing on the 7th September 1949 about Ivor Brown's book on Shakespeare, Shaw says: 'You describe Shakespeare as ambitious. What had so great a genius to aspire to? Hamlet's "I lack ambition" is a key-word. . . . You write of Will's fidelity to nature. You must bear in mind that he knew that acting and stage speech were (and are) the most artificial of all arts, and that what Hamlet urged on players was not to hold the mirror up to nature, but to make their excessively unnatural declamation *seem* natural and not "ham". . . . The Sonnets were best understood by Lord Alfred Douglas, who, like Mr W H, was adored for his personal beauty. Shakespeare's adoration is in the lump a nauseous mess of green-sickly drivel.' Then, talking of the Dark Lady of the Sonnets, Shaw says: 'I agree that she was probably dead when he wrote *Anthony and Cleopatra*; but as likely as not he had got over his infatuation for her. There is nothing so dead as a dead sexual passion.' He ends by describing himself as being 'among the most bardolatrous of all bardolators' and adds that

186

his earlier criticism of Shakespeare was caused by 'the fury and scurrility of the anti-Ibsen persecution, and the praise by the Press critics of Irving's and Daly's mutilations of Shakespeare's plays': it was this that made it 'necessary to debunk Shakespeare as well as extol Ibsen'.

Nothing could more clearly indicate the clarity of Shaw's mind and the power of his reasoning at the age of ninety-three.

His final illness was preceded by two falls in the garden. The first occurred early in the summer of 1950. 'After listening to the six o'clock news on the radio, he went into the garden,' Mrs Laden told me. 'I just happened to be near a window and saw him totter and fall into a hedge. He seemed embarrassed and glanced around him to make sure that no one was looking. I quickly drew back as I knew it would upset him if he saw me. Relieved at finding that no one was watching he picked himself up, dusted his clothes and walked on normally and rather nonchalantly, to the end of the garden.

'I said nothing for some days. Then, quite casually, as though I had just thought of it, I said: "I am a little worried, Mr Shaw. It's always possible for anyone of us to slip and fall in the garden. Would it be a good idea if I gave you this whistle I've got, to put in your pocket – then if by chance you happen to fall you could blow the whistle and I'd know where to find you and come along and help. Blow two or three blasts so that I shall be sure to hear it." He stared at me for a while, wondering, I suppose, if I had seen what happened earlier that week, or whether I just had Highland second-sight. Anyway he took the whistle, put it between his lips and tried it out. Then he smiled and stuffed it into his pocket.

'Occasionally in the last year or so he was slightly off colour. It did not happen often. But one morning when he came down at seven o'clock fully dressed as always, he looked very ill indeed and was not able to eat his breakfast. I suggested that he should lie down.

He said: "I'm not going upstairs." So I moved the sofa up to the fire and put down some blankets. "Lie down there," I said – and he did.

'I thought he ought to have a stimulant of some sort. But he didn't drink at all, as you know, and giving him alcohol in any form was just not possible. So I phoned Dr T C Probyn of the nearby village of Kimpton, described Mr Shaw's condition and told him what I had in mind. "Yes," he said. "Give him some whisky – about three ounces of whisky." "But, Doctor," I said, "he has never had a drop of whisky in his life. The problem is how am I going to get him to drink it without his knowing." A way round this had to be found and it came to me suddenly when I was preparing his lunch. I put three ounces of whisky into his soup.

'Would he be able to taste it? I wondered. I stood just outside the dining-room door so that I should hear if he called for it to be taken away. But to my relief he drank it all. I can't tell you how relieved I felt when I came in later and found that the soup dish had been drained to the last drop. I made him comfortable on the sofa and went out in his chocolate-coloured chauffeur-driven Lanchester to do some shopping. We used the big car for our purchases: when I went out on personal errands I used my little Corgi motor-scooter. When I bought that Mr Shaw insisted on giving me his old goggles, the ones he used when he was mad about motor-cycling. "You must use these," he said. They were very nice indeed with gold rims and I always used them.

'On my return to Shaw's Corner that afternoon I could hear the tapping of his typewriter and, going into the dining-room, I found him seated at the table, writing. He looked up and smiled. "I feel very well, you see," he said. After that I gave him three ounces of whisky in his soup quite often just to buck him up. Not being used to it he reacted quickly. It did him a lot of good and kept him going.

'I had planned to take a short holiday early in September. Mr Shaw seemed to sense this, for he said, "You're planning to go away for a few days, aren't you?" I said I was thinking of it. He was dejected, which I could quite understand. I told him that I would not be away long, that I would arrange everything and that the maids would look after him well. "You need a holiday of course," he said, and he insisted that I should travel in the Rolls to the station in London.

'On Friday, the 8th September, the day I was leaving, I went into the dining-room to say goodbye. He seemed a little restless and said: "I think you should leave your telephone number," which I did. He thanked me and added: "You see, I'm now a very old man."

'I went to Aberdeen where my home is. Two days later, on the Sunday evening, I had a phone-call from Dr Probyn to tell me that Mr Shaw had fallen in the garden and broken a bone. I said: "I am coming back at once. Will you tell Mr Shaw that?"

'The accident occurred shortly after six o'clock. Mr Shaw, for some reason – I don't know why, he usually went for a walk in the garden or in the village – went to the staircase and after climbing a few steps, noticed that the branch of a plum tree was broken. So he came down again to deal with it. He went into the dining-room where the garden tools were kept, selected a pair of secateurs and went out to deal with the broken branch. As he stood under it and grasped it, the branch, which was laden with plums, snapped and fell on him. The blow knocked him down and Dr Probyn found that he had broken his thigh bone.

'As there were no planes from Aberdeen on Sunday evening I took a train at 6.30 the next morning for Glasgow and flew from Renfrew to London, reaching Shaw's Corner within twenty-two and a half hours of the accident. Mr Shaw, who had already been operated on at the Luton and Dunstable Hospital, had not yet come round and it was heart-rending to see him lying there, quite lost and forlorn. The next day he looked at me with sad eyes and said in a very soft, pathetic voice, "Take me home." I said I would get him home as quickly as I could and that I would have a word with the matron at once. It was, of course, obvious that they would want him to stay there for a while. I explained this to him and assured him that I would not let them keep him there a moment longer than was absolutely necessary.

'Actually he was kept in the hospital for eighteen days, and every day, the moment I entered his room, his first words to me were always: "Take me home with you today." The broken femur was not the only trouble. Mr Shaw also had a prostate condition, of which I was aware although he tried to prevent my discovering it. He used to make sure that no one was about before slipping into the cloakroom, and at night he kept a little bowl under his bed and used to empty it himself in the morning, wash it and put it away.'

Silent about this before, she now revealed that she had known of it for months. 'You have been keeping a secret from me,' she said. 'What secret?' he enquired. She told him. He looked very sheepish, she says. 'At any rate, after fixing the broken femur with a pin, I believe that a prostate operation was suggested but Mr Shaw wouldn't hear of it. The real reason, I think, was that Mr Shaw had no wish to live: all his friends were dead and he felt it was time he went too.

'He was comfortable in the hospital,' Mrs Laden says. 'He had a room to himself and was very well looked after by the nurses. But he just didn't want to be there. It wasn't home. He was not really a difficult patient like his wife. But he had his little grumbles. Pointing to a nurse who had just gone out of the room, a fine-looking, buxom and kind girl, he said: "I don't want her here. She's very rough." I told him that was nonsense. And again: "I pay all this money here and they bring me my food on a tin tray. Take me home." I brought him his usual tray from the house the next morning and told them to use it in future. I also brought along his own bedsheets and pillow cases, because he found the hospital's cotton sheets too cold – his were of fine linen. "They come in," he complained, "and if they find I'm asleep, they say in a loud voice, 'Oh, you're asleep,' as though I had done something wrong. If, on the other hand, I happen to be awake, they say, 'Why aren't you asleep?' And they are always washing me. I told them, 'Antiques don't need so much washing.' " Winston Churchill, in America at the time, hearing of Shaw's accident, sent him some peaches from Florida.'

Despite Mrs Laden's persistent persuasion, the doctors were most reluctant to let him go home. 'It's much too early,' they said. 'You haven't the facilities there – nurses, appliances, diet and so on.' The surgeon, Mr L W Plewes, said: 'He needs elaborate care and extremely good nursing.' But Mrs Laden, moved by Shaw's incessant pleading, refused to surrender. 'I have gone into all that,' she said. 'I have two excellent nurses lined up – one for the night, the other for day nursing – and I'll get a third nurse if necessary. I shall go to John Bell and Croydon in Wigmore Street and convert the house into a hospital. I am sure you can see that psychologically it is most important for Mr Shaw to be in his own home. He hankers after it and it will do him a power of good if you will allow me to take him back.'

Many days were required to organise things. 'I had to engage the nurses and buy quite a lot of stuff – a bed-table, a wheel-chair for him and a trolley for the medicaments. The dining-room was converted into his bedroom, because it was on the ground floor, and I had his bed brought down. All the cushions in the house were assembled to make the bed really comfortable. The drawing-room was made into a recreation room for the nurses. His study was used as a medical store-room, with stacks of cotton wool and that sort of thing; and the nearby cloakroom was very handy for water.

'When the Press heard he was coming home they arrived in force with their cameras, and waited by the gate to photograph him. But I refused to allow it. His cheeks had got very sunken and his face looked like Death's head. "I am not going to let you photograph a dying man," I said. He was brought back in an ambulance and I had a large piece of tarpaulin held up like a screen to shield him from the cameras when he was brought out. "You wait," I told the pressmen. "Let him have two or three hours' rest, then you can go in." They were most co-operative and agreed to wait.

'As he was taken into his familiar dining-room, now his bedroom, Mr Shaw's emaciated face beamed. "Back in your ain haime," I said, using the Scottish form which he himself sometimes adopted to tease me. He smiled and said: "Oh, what a relief to be home. I'm glad to be out of that bloody place. It is far better to be with the Devil you know than the Devil you don't know."

'He made very good progress and seemed to be getting better every day. Dr Probyn came daily to see him. I had discussed his diet with the hospital dietician in great detail and told the two nurses that it would have to be most rigidly adhered to. The whisky I had been giving him in his soup was added right up to the end. I think Mr Shaw had by now begun to suspect this, for he said to me one day: "I know you play tricks with me, Mrs Laden." I was taken aback. "In what way?" I asked. "Well, look at me," he said. "I feel better every day." He didn't laugh. He was very serious.

'I had been told by Mr Plewes that we must get Mr Shaw up every day. In addition to the pin in the broken thigh bone, he had a metal tube all the way down his leg to keep it firm. "He must stand on that leg every day," Mr Plewes said. We saw to that. We held him up as he walked from his bed to the chair.

'During this period of convalescence, which lasted a month, he appeared to be quite cheerful. Every evening at six o'clock the radio was switched on and after the news he listened to the BBC's excellent music on the

Third Programme. Beethoven, Mozart and Brahms brought him immense enjoyment.

'One evening I was baking in the kitchen, my hands covered with flour up to the elbow, when the nurse told me that Mr Shaw wanted to see me. I said: "I wonder what he wants?" Mischievously she replied: "He's going to propose to you." "He has left it a bit late in the day," I replied. I washed my hands and went to him. His bright blue eyes, still perfectly clear, twinkled as he said: "You know my time is short. Who is the undertaker?" I thought I'd play it light. "For me or for yourself?" I asked. "You know perfectly well who it's for." I said nothing. "Why you?" he enquired. "Because," I replied, still evading the real issue, "I'm worn out the way you are going on." He noticed my smile. "Is it . . . "? He hesitated and mentioned a name which I couldn't place; then after some reflection I said, "That's your tailor. If you're thinking of the undertaker his name is Mr Blow of Welwyn."

'Mr Shaw said: "I want to be put into a plain wooden box. No furbelows. I'm going into the furnace and that's all I want." He made me write all this and a lot more down and made me promise that I would carry out all his wishes. "I want you to get me out of this house at once. I don't want you looking at me after I'm dead." '

A night or two later someone telephoned from the BBC. 'We know that Mr Shaw listens to the Third Programme and enjoys the music. We should like to play for him something he would specially like to hear – a symphony by Beethoven or a concerto by Mozart perhaps.' Mrs Laden said it was most thoughtful and kind of them and she was sure Mr Shaw would appreciate it. 'I'll go and ask him.' Informed of it, Shaw merely stared at her. 'The man is on the phone, waiting for your answer. What shall I tell him?' 'Tell him,' Shaw said, 'to play The Old Cow Died.' Mrs Laden left the bedside puzzled. 'I don't know if that was some old Irish song or he was just trying to be funny,' she told me. It was an old music-hall song.

Shaw had very few visitors now. I was one of the last to see him, as has been described in an earlier chapter. Lady Astor called two days later, on the Sunday, forty-eight hours or so before his death. It was odd that he should at that time think of entertaining her with a story that for some reason had come bubbling up out of the depths of his memory. He said: 'A very wealthy Italian gentleman had invited a large number of guests to dinner in his lovely house in Rome. While they were sipping their short drinks before the meal was announced, the butler came up and whispered something to the host, who changed colour and rose from his chair. Turning to his guests he said: "I'm afraid I must ask you to leave. I have just learned that my wife is in bed with a man." The guests mumbled their commiseration, bowed in farewell and were struggling into their coats when the butler returned and spoke to the host again. "Stop! Stop!" the Italian gentleman called to his guests. "The man with my wife has apologised. So we can now go in to dinner." '

Shaw said to Dr Probyn the next day: 'I should like you to mingle my ashes after the cremation with Mrs Shaw's and scatter them in the grounds of this house.' He then sent for Mrs Laden and thanked her for staying with him and looking after him. That night, in the small hours, Shaw went into a coma. One of the nurses hurried to Mrs Laden to tell her.

'The coma lasted twenty-six hours. I sent for the undertaker the next morning, realising that this was the end and pointed out to him that Mr Shaw was a very tall man. On the Thursday morning, the 2nd November, at one minute to five o'clock, Mr Shaw died. The Press was waiting and I went out to inform them.

'The rector, Mr Davies, held a service in the house, which was attended by the village people: it was such a lovely service; and then, at Mr Shaw's own express wish, his body was taken to the Chapel of Rest at Welwyn. The cremation was at Golders Green crematorium. It was a mild day, fitfully sunny, and there was a vast crowd of people there, but admission to the service was by ticket. Miss Blanche Patch, his secretary, was there, of course, as well as Lady Astor, the nurses, the entire domestic staff and myself. On the day the ashes were scattered in the garden it poured with rain.'

I had seen when I was in the house a few days earlier a photograph of the interior of St Patrick's Cathedral in Dublin, showing a wide expanse of floor-space in the foreground. Mrs Laden told me then that Shaw had often pointed to it and said: 'That's where I want to be buried,' possibly because Swift was buried quite near it. Knowing that he had already arranged to have his ashes scattered with his wife's in the garden of his house at Ayot St Lawrence, I wondered what had made him change his mind. But he reverted to his earlier plan just before his death and Dr Probyn carried it out.

18
Money

SHAW LEFT THE enormous sum of £367,233 13s 0d; the net figure was £301,585 7s 5d. It was one of the largest fortunes ever left by a writer.

The thought of taxation and eventual death-duties had worried him to the end. Talking to Hesketh Pearson, who called to see him twelve months before he died, Shaw kept wailing that he would have to pay £140,000 in taxation during the coming year. Death-duty on the money he left was considerably larger than that: it was estimated to be £180,571 1s 4d, but this was not the final figure. The value of his copyrights had to be taken into account and it was assessed at £443,500. When this was added to the sum Shaw had actually left, the revised death-duties amounted to £524,000 – and there was not that much money to pay it. Shaw's estate was in consequence in debt to the State, and it took six years for the royalties from his plays and his books to clear this. Only then was it possible to consider the bequests he had set out in his will.

The personal bequests were few: cash sums or annuities were provided for his secretary, Miss Blanche Patch, for Mrs Laden, and for his entire domestic staff – chauffeur, gardener, bee-keeper and maids. Not many relatives had to be considered as most of them were already dead. Those who remained received small bequests.

The rest of the money he wanted for devising a new alphabet of about forty letters so that English could be written phonetically: this had been a lifelong ambition; but, forseeing that it might be disputed in a court of law, he provided an alternative, namely that the money should be divided in equal shares among three institutions – the British Museum, which had been his only library and had been constantly used by him during his early years in London; the National Gallery of Ireland, where he claimed he had learned all he knew about art, which was not much, although for a short time in his earliest excursion into journalism he had served as an art critic; and the Royal Academy of Dramatic Art, which he hoped would continue to train actors and actresses to perform in his plays.

In the years since his death the income from his books and, chiefly, from his plays has far exceeded anything he earned from them in his lifetime. His plays are constantly being revived, occasionally as many as two or three of them are on at the same time in London, New York and elsewhere. But the greatest source of income has come from *My Fair Lady* – the musical play, and later film, based on *Pygmalion*. Whether he would have agreed to this being done had he lived is open to conjecture. We know that he was enraged when his play *Arms and the Man* was, without his consent, presented as a musical on the German stage and later performed in many other countries as *The Chocolate Soldier*. That was in the early twenties. Shaw went to see it in London and regarded it as a travesty of his play; he said, however, that he would not take any action if certain sections were deleted: and he refused to accept any money from it. But when an American arrived at his flat in Adelphi Terrace and told him that he had bought the film-rights of *The Chocolate Soldier*, Shaw took a firmer stand. Nothing must be quoted from his dialogue in *Arms and the Man*, nor must his name be connected with it in any way, he insisted, otherwise legal action would be taken. It was, however, not Shaw but the American impresario who brought an action against Shaw for making it impossible for him to produce the film. The Court ruled that the American had no case.

Shaw told me on his deathbed that *Pygmalion* was not a romantic play, 'not a love story'. Had he adhered to that view he would not have allowed *My Fair Lady* to be made.

I discussed this with Rex Harrison one evening at his villa at Portofino. Rex's eyes narrowed and he said after a moment: 'I think Shaw would have liked my interpretation of Professor Higgins. When I was invited to play in *My Fair Lady* I had doubts about taking on the rôle. I thought I'd better look at Leslie Howard's interpretation of Higgins and I saw the film of *Pygmalion*. I admired Leslie as an actor, but I felt that his interpretation of the rôle was wrong.'

I then told Rex what Shaw had told me. 'I too felt that Leslie was much too weak,' he said. 'Charles Laughton would certainly have been strong – much, much better than Leslie Howard, but he would not have been right.

'I decided to make a very close and careful study of the part. I went about with Shaw's play in my pocket and read it again and again to get the exact meaning of Shaw's words – of every syllable of every word, since Shaw attached immense importance to syllables; and it became quite obvious to me that Higgins would at all times have to be the boss in his scenes with Eliza Doolittle. He had to be dictatorial, never gentle and kind.

'Eventually I began to realise that Higgins was really Shaw himself and I decided to play the part as Shaw without the beard. Having come to this conclusion I saw the film of *Pygmalion* once again and realised that I was right. I think Shaw would have approved of my interpretation of Higgins. I feel in fact that Shaw would have liked the film too, except perhaps the last two minutes of it.'

The last scene in *My Fair Lady* shows Higgins coming into his study. He walks around thoughtfully and turns on the recording of Eliza's voice. His hat still on his head, he sits on a stool and listens. It says: 'Well, here I am

198

ready to pay, not asking any favour – and he treats me as if I were dirt.'

Eliza walks softly into the room and after a while turns off the machine and says: 'I washed my face and hands before I come, I did.'

Higgins straightens up, then leans back with a contented sigh and tips his hat forward until it covers his face. Then he says softly: 'Eliza? Where the devil are my slippers?'

The importance of every syllable of every word began for Shaw in 1884 when he realised the need for exact articulation as a public speaker. Nearly half a century later, in 1930, Lord Reith, the Director General of the BBC, invited Shaw to be Chairman of the Spoken English Advisory Committee to guide the announcers on the correct pronunciation of words.

'All our announcers,' Reith told me, 'had to go through a school, and GBS, who spoke a purer English than the average Englishman, was extremely helpful to us and rendered a considerable service to the BBC.'

Shaw was also an ex-officio member of the BBC's General Advisory Council. When he resigned seven years later, because he was going on a tour of South America, his letter to Reith characteristically suggested that the Council 'should be reconstituted with an age limit of thirty' – he was himself seventy-eight at the time – 'and have a few taxi-drivers on it. The young people *won't* pronounce like the old dons. . . . Are we to dictate to the mob or allow the mob to dictate to us?'

In the ten years following the Court's decision on Shaw's will regarding the reform of the alphabet, the British Museum, by investing its one-third share of Shaw's royalties and using only the interest, has an accumulated capital of nearly £1 million, the bulk of it from *My Fair Lady*.

Shaw's bleatings about having no money and being a poor man have led many to believe that he was mean.

This is not true. Having known acute poverty until middle age and faced even after that for many more years with uncertainty about his income, he was understandably careful. He appeared to be haunted all his life by a fear of the workhouse, which he knew only too well when he was a vestryman and councillor at St Pancras. 'I would hate to be poor,' he said more than once to Mrs Laden, to me and to others. 'I couldn't bear it again, I just couldn't go back to poverty'; and so he deluded himself into believing that if he earned more money the higher tax would eat into what he already had, which, of course, was nonsense, for if he was left, after taxation, with as little as sixpence in the pound, he would still have 1,000 sixpences or £25 out of every additional £1,000.

But generosity was not unknown. What he gave was given secretly, as though by stealth. 'He seemed ashamed at times,' Mrs Laden told me, 'of being generous with his money.' Perhaps he feared that if it got known he would be overwhelmed with demands for help. 'I remember an occasion,' Mrs Laden says, 'when I picked up his batch of letters for the post. I found among them one that was stamped but unsealed and in it was a cheque for £15. I took it to him and asked if he wanted it to be posted. He looked very sheepish. "I've had a letter from a silly woman whom I don't even know, asking me for £25 to buy a typewriter. Why should I give it to her?" He licked the flap of the envelope and pasted it down, leaving the £15 cheque inside: if she didn't get all she asked for, at any rate she got quite a substantial part of it, enough to buy a good second-hand typewriter.'

I know he helped authors who were in need. John Stewart Collis, the Irish poet and writer, told me: 'I was very young and hard up at the time and I wrote and asked Shaw if he would help me. He sent me a cheque for £50 at once. Many years later, when I sought his help again, he sent this letter: "One reads in the papers that I am a multi-millionaire and that I have never sent a less fortunate author away empty (actually I seem to spend my life bawling No, No, No) when they appeal to me for help: we should be destitute in a month or so if our hearts had not long ago become millstones.'' Attached to the letter was a cheque for £10.'

'Mind you, I can't say he enjoyed parting with money,' says Mrs Laden. 'Giving was one thing: I know of many instances when he helped others, but he always did it surreptitiously. He was generous to me. He doubled my salary again and again, off his own bat. But if I took a bill to him for, let us say, £20 he'd make a fuss – he always did. An American professor who admired him wrote at the end of the war to say that he was sending him a liquidiser as he knew Mr Shaw enjoyed fruit-juices. He was delighted and almost every day used to say: "I wonder if it will arrive today." At last it came and he was overjoyed. But one morning some weeks later he sent for me. I found him standing erect as a soldier by the fireplace and in his hand was a bill. He said: "Have you taken my name for £39?" I was flabbergasted. I said: "You know me better than that. What do you mean?" He handed me a bill from Fortnum and Mason marked "For goods £39". "We'll soon find out about this," I said. I phoned Fortnum's and was told that it was for a liquidiser that had been ordered for Mr Shaw by some local friends. I told Mr Shaw of this, but he said nothing – not even a word to say he was sorry he had misjudged me. I was furious. I said: "Unless I am completely trusted I am not going to stay. You had better find someone else whom you can trust." He remained silent, so I left the room.

'He went down to his hut at the end of the garden and typed out a letter to me in which he said: "Your atomic bomb exploded on my breakfast table this morning. Are you engaged to be married? If so I am not surprised and must accept your notice. If not, is there anything I can do? You are of course too good for the very dull job; but think it over unless you have some definite plan. You are too young and energetic to settle down in retirement;

201

and as you will housekeep anyhow, it will be actually cheaper to keep my house than your own. No doubt you can better yourself; but I cannot – G Bernard Shaw."

'I remember the occasion when he lost his wallet while walking through the wood just beyond his hut. A child found it and brought it to him. Mr Shaw asked "How did you know it was my wallet?" – "Because," said the child, "your old woman's picture is in it." I was standing by him and said: "Shall I give him £5?" Mr Shaw said: "No. I'll give him £10 for his honesty." He was not a mean man. But bills were always scrutinised most carefully. He bought an adding machine but he found he couldn't cope with it. A man was called in to give him lessons on how to use it, but he found it impossible to handle, so he passed it on to me. "You are an infallible counter, Mrs Laden," he said. "See if you can deal with this thing." Right up to the end he was conscious of money. After his fall, on my return from Scotland, the maid gave me his wallet together with the pens, keys and other things he had in his pockets. I kept them until his homecoming from the hospital. As I handed them to him he said: "I had £29 and seven shillings in the wallet." "Yes," I said. "Here it is – all of it. What do you want me to do with the money?" "Put it into your housekeeping," he said. He knew exactly how much he had. Even in the last week of his life he went through all the household accounts to the last detail.'

A most revealing light was shed on his attitude to money in a letter to Mrs Patrick Campbell, written in December 1912 when he was deeply in love with her; they did not quarrel until many months later. He wrote: 'Shall I tell you the calculations I have been going over in my head ever since you became ill? Listen.

'Money. She must have money to go on with. Has she any? Let me see. £116 a week all through the run of *Bella Donna*. Half to the bankers to pay off debts. That leaves £58 a week going to her credit. But it also proves that the bankers must have allowed her to overdraw recklessly. For that the bank manager ought to be sacked; for there are no securities: she told me she had saved nothing. Unless the bank has insured her life, the manager's conduct in permitting the overdraft is un-businesslike to the verge of malversation. Therefore either the manager or the firm (or more probably all of them) is in love with her. That being so, they may say "Perish the bank: let her have the last sovereign in the safe rather than she should have a moment's anxiety." In their place I should have that impulse.

'But business is business: in practice there is a limit to all overdrafts. That limit may be approaching – may be already reached – must be near enough to cause some anxiety. Are there friends – for pride is no use: when you *must* have money you must take it or raise it – must, must, must, must, MUST. DD – Saville' – (a reference to two of her friends) – 'who is there? But if they didn't offer and insist she might go to a money-lender. She would. Delicacy: that's the difficulty: a woman is visibly spending money like water and earning nothing; and people talk of delicacy! Thank God *I* have no delicacy – no good taste – she said so – oh sweet revenge, to turn myself, like Jupiter with Danae, into a shower of gold! Only, I haven't gold enough: I'm not rich; and there's Mama and Lucy and others; and I am a member of a firm, Charlotte & Co. No; it doesn't run to a shower.

'How much will she need? No: I must be prudent: how little can she scrape through with? There's the rent, the Xmas quarter. Then Xmas boxes, bills, nurses, doctors. Of course she is saving a lot by being in bed: no dressing, no taxis. The thought that there might be a bill-of-sale on that piano is like a dagger. Insistent problem: how much will make her quite free from anxiety until she is up again? And how much can I afford? No use pretending to be opulent: I'm not. The Xmas fortnight: would £250 get her over it?

'Oh God! to offer Stella a filthy little £250! I spit on myself. But she says she can't keep money – gives it to whoever asks her – despicable weakness! Better perhaps dole out a little at a time: other fortnights will follow Xmas. How much can I afford? Ass! why ask that question over and over again? You know perfectly well that you want to give her a thousand pounds. Very well: put your cheque book in your pocket and go to her and ask her. If she does not want it there is no harm done: you are no use: that is all. If she does want it, and will not take it: there are ways – artful ways – guileful ways – but the simple way is sincere, and will do. True, she will suddenly realise that I am, after all, a stranger to her; but what of that! she is not a stranger to me; and she has forfeited the right to refuse, because she has given money, and would give it to me if I wanted it. Can I seriously believe that she will say "Insolent stranger; you have violated my pride, my privacy, my feeling that I must be a star and not a candle lighted by a man with a match. Ring the bell; and have yourself turned out." I wasn't a bit afraid of that. . . .

'My grandfather used to say that no living man, prince or pauper, could refuse a five-pound note if you crackled it under his nose. Why did I not get a thousand-pound note and crackle it under your nose? Say what you will, there's something dignified about a thousand-pound note. Wouldn't you like to take it and burn it before my face? *Quel geste!* I could take the number, swear to the burning, get another one, and crackle that too.

'Stella, if those bankers – no: don't be angry: I only say IF, IF, IF, IF. And so enough of that. Only, dearest, if you ever want anything ever so little, remember, crackle, crackle, crackle, crackle. If it pleased you to give to the Ragbag, think of what it would be to me – but no no no: it would not be the same: it would be like nothing on earth. Oh, to call it an obligation! to thank one, in that high heroic way, for NOTHING! to deny me – oh, yes, yes, yes: I am making a lot of it; I have, as you say, no taste. But if I *had* any taste, I should have risked making it impossible ever to ask you anything. Was not that a sacrifice? No: for I have had everything – the sun and moon and all the stars of heaven.'

We do not know if he gave her that money, or any money at that time. What we do know is that Charlotte, his wife, was financially independent, so was his mother; as for his sister Lucy, to whom he refers as a dependant of his, she had not spoken to him for years and was certainly not receiving support from him.

But there were many other acts of kindness through the earlier years of his life, which involved the expenditure of a great deal of his time though not of his money, for he had none then; and of time he always gave most readily. There was Molly Tompkins, a young American actress, who came to London in 1921 with her sculptor husband, who was busy designing a Shavian theatre with carvings on its stone façade to represent Shaw's creative thoughts. They called on Shaw and a warm friendship developed. He took them around London, for long walks in the countryside and wrote a great many letters to Molly right up to the year before his death. These letters, diverting, instructive, were often long – he must have spent endless hours over some of them. In one of the earliest he pointed out that no 'gentleman' in England should be addressed on the envelope as 'Mr', but should have 'Esquire or Esq.' after his name. The letters have since been published in book form (most of them reproduced in Shaw's own handwriting) by Molly's son Peter Tompkins.

An approach of a very different kind was made by Arthur Askey, who wanted to represent Shaw in an amusing music-hall sketch. On the Lord Chamberlain's insistence Shaw's consent was required, and this he refused to give. Very dejected, Arthur Askey, walking past Whitehall Court one morning, decided on an impulse to go in and speak to Shaw about it. 'It was the most frightful cheek,' he told me. 'I did not know him. I rang the front-door bell and asked his secretary if I could see him. She said he was very busy. But from one of the rooms I heard his voice enquiring "Who is it?" and when she gave my name, to my delight he said: "Ask him to come in." I was taken into his study and was greeted most affably. He said: "I have often listened to you on the radio. You make me laugh a lot. What have you come to see me about?" I noticed the script of my sketch was lying on his desk, so I pointed to it and said: "It's about that." He picked it up, read the first two lines aloud and said: "This piece of schoolboy rubbish?" I said it was the highlight of our show, to which he replied: "I wonder what the lowlight is like." At this I said: "Schoolboy rubbish, Mr Shaw, is my livelihood."

'After a while he smiled. "Shakespeare," he said, "who was no mean writer, has often been represented on the stage. He isn't here to defend himself. I have been impersonated too. I took my mother once to see a show at a music-hall. My beard was red then and the man who took me off made me laugh a lot. But my mother didn't laugh at all. She merely said: 'What was that silly old devil going on about?'" ' Thus encouraged I asked: "Can I do it then, Mr Shaw?" He smiled again. "As I won't be there what's there to stop you?" So we did it. The sketch represented an encounter between Shaw and Shakespeare with "not bloody likely" dragged in, inevitably.'

Ronald Gow, the playwright and Wendy Hiller's husband, tells me that in his earlier years, when he was associated with an amateur dramatic society near Manchester, he had sent a telegram to Shaw asking: 'Can we play *Candida*?' Shaw replied on a postcard: 'I don't know, but you can try'; and he went on to suggest that they should turn themselves into professionals because by doing so the sum payable to the author would be only 7s 6d, whereas as amateurs they would be required to pay as much as five guineas. 'We did that,' Gow told me, 'and were delighted to get it so cheap.'

Postscript

That Shaw was one of the world's greatest dramatists cannot be disputed even if it is argued that not more than a dozen or so of his plays are worth reviving.

But his influence as a political force, an economist and a philosopher will be questioned by many. He did not create, but was caught up by almost every stream of new thought and boldly waded to the very forefront bearing the appropriate banner. That many fell in behind him is due to the pungency of his phrase and the ridicule he directed on conventions that were already dying hard.

But by the time he was approaching the age of seventy when most people have nothing to lose but their prejudices, Shaw reversed that process. A radical all his life, he began to find fault with the time-honoured theory of equality and bestowed his blessing on such men and Supermen as Mussolini, Stalin and Hitler. Democracy seemed to him to be inoperable and needed a dictator at the helm – even if democracy was destroyed in the process.

How deep then was his faith, how far down did the roots of his beliefs go? Or did they lie merely upon the surface of his brilliant phrases and scintillating arguments?

Appendix

Shaw's Vegetarian Meals – with Menus

Breakfast
Porridge, grape-fruit, toast, marmalade or marrow jam, very
weak white coffee. Shredded Wheat was the only cereal he
liked.

Lunch
Various soups, followed by a bowl of raw fresh vegetables
grated and covered with mango chutney.

The main dish was one of the following:
Vegetable Charlotte served with Tartare sauce.
Vegetable curry served with Bengal chutney.
Vegetable patties served with cheese sauce.
Baked potatoes in their jackets served with butter and
Parmesan.
French beans baked with double cream and nutmeg.
Stuffed grilled aubergines with fried onions and parsley sauce.
Asparagus boiled with oiled butter.
Casserole of Brussels sprouts served with cheese, tomato and
onions.
Carrot croquettes served with lemon sauce.
Creamed celeriac served with cranberry sauce.
Stuffed mushrooms served with tomato purée.
Buttered cucumber served with savoury sauce.
Sweet corn served with apple sauce.
Stuffed tomatoes served with double cream sauce.
Stuffed green or red peppers served with cucumber sauce.
Cauliflower-au-gratin served with Parmesan cheese.
Cheese sausages served with pineapple rings.

Baked stuffed marrow served with redcurrent jelly.
Savoury stuffed apple served with mint jelly.
Cheese pudding served with rhubarb sauce.
Nut roast served with rice and onion.
Cheese soufflé served with sultanas or raisins.
Buck rarebit served with French toast and tomatoes.
Macaroni and cheese served with prepared prunes.
Spaghetti fritters served with tomato and apple sauce.
Cheese omelettes served with tomato sauce.
Curried savoury rice served with chestnut sauce.
Lentil cutlets served with onions and Tartare sauce.
Croquettes of macaroni served with cream and herb sauce.
Cheese Strudel served with cream, cheese, nuts and poppy seeds.
Baked banana and tomato served with Cumberland sauce.
Walnut and potato pie served with chives and walnut
  ketchup.
Potato curls served with onion and ample grated cheese to
  cover curls.
Casserole of broad beans served with mint and a cup of cream.
Cheese puffs served with chopped almonds and sultanas.
Spanish onion, stuffed, served with chestnuts, cress, lemon
  slices and tomato.
Cheese rissoles rolled in oatmeal served with parsley sauce.
Risotto served baked with whole tomatoes with mint sauce.
Cutlets of rice served with mashed turnips and tomato sauce.
Baked haricot beans served with nut oil and cream in parsley
  sauce.
Cheese fondeau served with walnuts, almonds, celery,
  mustard and celery sauce.
Vegetarian sweetbreads served with parsnip, artichokes,
  cheese, onion and mace.
Mock chicken patties served with onions, walnuts, mace and
  bread sauce.
Vol-au-vent of cauliflower served with spiced turnips, braised
  onion and cheese sauce.
Croquettes of split peas served with celery, tomatoes, mush-
  room and cream sauce.
Potato ring, the centre filled with hot diced vegetables served
  with tomato sauce.
Walnut and potato pie served with chopped chives and
  walnut ketchup.

Grilled tomatoes served with buttered toast, horseradish and cress, parsley.

Steamed mushrooms served with half a cup of cream poured over the mushrooms before serving and French toast.

Potato and cheese turnovers served with wholemeal flour, cream cheese, onions, chives, milk, vegetable oil and cream.

Most of these dishes were served with a potato dish, such as chipped, mashed, roast, baked, Duchess, puffkins, game, fritters, Lyonnaise.

Sweets
Various kinds of fresh fruit, nuts and dates, cream cheese or Stilton or some choice sweets.

Ices, sundaes and mousse were greatly favoured by Mr Shaw.

ICES – Rich cream ice, vanilla ice, apricot ice, blackcurrant ice, strawberry ice, chestnut ice or marshmallow ice.

WATER ICES – Lemon, orange, cranberry, rose made from fresh roses.

MOUSSE – Coffee, chocolate, strawberry, vanilla or lemon.

SUNDAES – Chocolate nut, fruit, pineapple, pêche melba, peach or apricot, chopped nuts or maple date.

DRINK – Passion fruit or fresh blackcurrant, also barley water and lemon, made at home.

Dinners
A very light meal.

Soup (various), or melon with preserved ginger, or avocado pear with vinegar or Worcester sauce, followed by compôte of fresh fruit and cream, sometimes baked apples, very seldom cooked fruits.

Lastly, white coffee and cream.

In the summer months for dinner salad dishes were served instead of soup.

Salad Dishes
AVOCADO AND ORANGE – Lettuce, pear sliced, also orange sliced and prepared with mayonnaise – a delicious salad.

CUCUMBER – Cucumber, vinegar, paprika, sugar, parsley, cream or yoghourt.

FRENCH TOMATO – Large, ripe tomatoes, shallots, chopped parsley with French dressings.

CHEESE – Black Diamond cheese, lettuce, cucumber, caraway seeds, oil and vinegar.

ENDIVE (SPANISH) – Endive, lemon, garlic, clove, green and black olives, tomato, red pepper, salt, sugar, oil, vinegar.

POTATO – Cooked potato cubes, green onion, celery stalks, parsley, mayonnaise.

RUSSIAN – Cooked mixed vegetables, potato, beetroot, oil, vinegar.

RAISIN CRISP – Golden raisins, shredded cabbage, crushed pineapple, lettuce, paprika (dressing – thick cream, sugar, mustard, Worcester sauce, vinegar, beaten till thick).

His bread was always baked at home. He would not eat bread with a raising agent.

Mr Shaw did not drink tea at any time. A glass of milk was taken in its place.

MENUS

And here are the methods for preparing these dishes.

Vegetable Sausages
Boil 1 or 2 carrots, 2 onions, 1 parsnip. Chop all fine and prepare ¼ lb yeɪɪow peas, pound well, add vegetables and chopped parsley and tiny piece of chopped garlic and 2 oz breadcrumbs. Add seasoning, make into sausages with one whisked egg. Then dip egg and breadcrumbs and fry in boiling vegetable oil.

Vegetable Pie
Peel and slice potatoes, mushrooms, tomatoes and onions. Season well, add a little water, put in a pie dish. Top with a little broken-up butter, cover with a rich short pastry, bake for 1 hour.

Vegetable Sweetbreads
Stew 1 parsnip, 1 onion, 1 Jerusalem artichoke, a pinch of mace, and seasoning. When cooked cut into slices and place on top of each a piece of cheddar cheese of same size, lay them on thick slices of buttered toast and put in a quick oven until

cheese becomes soft and slightly brown. While this is cooking thicken the milk that the vegetables were stewed in, with butter and flour. Add some chopped parsley, and pour over sweetbreads.

Mock Chicken Patties
1 teacup shelled and grated walnuts, 1 cup breadcrumbs, 1 grated onion, 1 teaspoon mace, $\frac{1}{2}$ oz butter, 1 teaspoon flour, 1 teacup cream. Add seasoning. Mix all ingredients together and simmer for 15 mins. Make puff pastry cases and fill. Serve hot with a creamy bread sauce.

Rice and Lentil Cutlets
The lentils, like all cereals, must be soaked overnight, but every scrap of moisture must be removed before the other ingredients are added.

Boil the lentils and then the rice until quite tender. Cut up 1 onion and 2 cloves of garlic, chop very fine. Add a little tarragon, thyme and parsley. Mix well together, season well. Bind and shape into cutlets, egg and breadcrumb. Fry in vegetable oil until a nice brown. Serve with tomato sauce.

Tomatoes à la Bengal
Cut some bread into thick slices, cut into rounds, fry until crisp, drain thoroughly, keep hot. Peel about 4 tomatoes, cut into thick slices, season well, add a little curry powder. Pour a little melted butter over each crouton, cook in a moderate oven for 10 mins. Now spread croutons with chopped chutney, place tomatoes on top. Serve with a nice Cumberland sauce, very hot.

Savoury Rice
Boil the best Patna rice until tender, drain and put in colander. Run cold water through it until every grain is quite separated: let it get quite cold. Have ready a good helping of butter in a frying pan. Add rice, onion, tomato, also $\frac{1}{4}$ lb of the large Australian raisins, cleaned and chopped, 1 dessert apple, fine chopped, and 1 tablespoon of demerara sugar. Keep moving this mixture in pan. Serve very hot piled up in a very hot dish.

Cauliflower-au-Gratin

Boil the cauliflower most carefully. The flower must be whole and dish it standing upright in a basin dish. Pour a very good white sauce (thick) and when off the fire add a cup of cream. Sprinkle a good helping of Parmesan and breadcrumbs, or have ready a sauce prepared by thickening 1 pt of strained stewed tomatoes and add to this sauce half a cup of cream.

Stuffed Sweet Peppers

Cut into halves lengthwise, remove pith and boil for 5 mins. Stuff with savoury rice or spaghetti, dressed in cheese, also chopped apple. Put in a well-greased casserole, cook gently for 20 mins in a moderate oven. Otherwise the halves can be fastened together with toothpicks and fried in batter.

Vegetable Soufflé

Break up cauliflower into sprigs, cook for 10 mins in salt water. Make ½ pt white sauce, add yolks of 2 eggs, grated cheese, half a teaspoon mustard, and chop a few chives, then fold in stiffly beaten whites of the eggs. Put in a soufflé dish. Bake for half an hour.

Nut Roast

Take 1 cup of nuts, 1 cup of breadcrumbs, put them through a nut mill. Mix them well, add 1 cup of boiled rice, a sprinkle of sage and thyme, a good grating of onion, 1 teaspoon of salt, a ¼ teaspoon of pepper, and 1 oz melted butter. Moisten with a cup of boiled water. Dissolve 1 teaspoon Marmite and add this. Mould together and place in a greased dish. Bake in oven, basting with a little fat. Serve with roast potatoes.

Scalloped Mushrooms

Sauté 1 lb fresh cleaned and peeled mushrooms. Make 1 pt white sauce, add ½ grated onion. Grease a casserole and place a layer of mushrooms, adding a few breadcrumbs, then place in layers alternately. Pour over a little of the sauce, then add to the remainder of the sauce the stiffly whisked white of an egg, also a ¼ pt of thick cream. Pour this on the dish and sprinkle with crumbs. Bake in a moderate oven for 20 mins.

Potato Curls

Wash and peel potatoes (large), cutting round and round as though peeling an apple. Have ready 2 pans of boiling fat. Throw into one pan and remove when they begin to brown, drain thoroughly and throw them into second pan to finish browning and to soften sufficiently. Drain on greaseproof. Serve piled up on a napkin on a hot dish. Sprinkle with salt or with Parmesan.

Potato Puffkins

Make rolls or balls of mashed potatoes. Dip into a little melted fat, then roll in grated cheese seasoned with a little mustard and salt. Cook under gril¹ or in hot oven.

All cereals must be washed and soaked overnight; for soups – use the water in which they have been soaked in the soup, together with the cereals.

ICES

Rose Ice

Pick a bunch of fresh roses, thoroughly clean in cold water, then put petals into 1 pt of boiling water. Add 5 oz of sugar and keep covered very tightly. Strain when liquid is cooked, colour with a few drops of carmine red, and add 2 drops of eau-de-Cologne, and freeze.

Apricot Ice

Strain juice from a tin of apricots, put through a strainer enough sieved apricots to give ½ pt of pulp. Then mix ½ pt of juice with pulp, adding 4 oz of sugar. Add yolk of egg, and beat until thick. Place in freezing tray for about 3 hours then stir through with a fork to break it up. Return to tray and finish freezing.

Chestnut Ice

Blanch and remove skins of 1 lb chestnuts. Cook in a little milk, pass through sieve. Make a syrup with ¾ pt of water and 12 oz of sugar. Add now 4 well-beaten eggs, stirring in gradually until the mixture is cold. Finally add ¾ pt of thick cream, adding 4 oz chopped glacé cherries. Freeze.

Marshmallow Ice

Cut 16 to 20 marshmallows into small pieces with a pair of scissors, dip scissors frequently in hot water. Heat ¼ pt milk. When hot add marshmallows. Stir well. When dissolved add 1 teaspoon vanilla, then leave mixture until firm, then fold in ½ pt of thick cream. Place in freezing tray. Leave until frozen.

Acknowledgements

I AM INDEBTED to a large number of people, many of whom knew Shaw far better than I did: they were generous enough to give me a great deal of their time and to recount their impressions of various aspects of his life and thought, his gaiety and humour, his warmth and friendliness.

To some of them, who are no longer with us, I talked in the thirties during the years leading up to the war. One of these, H G Wells, talked of him reluctantly, answering the questions I asked and elaborating a little; another, Sir Cedric Hardwicke, always spoke of him with immense admiration and affection when we lunched together at the Savage Club, to which we both belonged; Lennox Robinson, the Irish playwright, who went with me to China to speak at the centenary of Shaw's birth in 1956; Vivien Leigh in a brief talk on my return from China; and Sir Jacob Epstein a few days after Shaw's death: I have drawn in all these instances on the notes I made during those years.

With Bertrand Russell I talked early in 1952: we spoke of many things and Shaw figured conspicuously in our talk.

Of the many others who drew on their memories of Shaw the most notable were Dame Sybil Thorndike, her husband Sir Lewis Casson, Dame Rebecca West and her husband, Henry Andrews, Miles Malleson, Wendy Hiller and her husband, Ronald Gow, Joyce Grenfell, Greer Garson, Kingsley Martin, Ivor Brown, Lord Reith, Ellen Pollock, Mrs Margaret Cole and Feliks Topolski, all of whom knew him well over the years.

To Dame Laura Knight, who painted a portrait of Shaw one summer at Malvern shortly before the war; Rex Harrison, who worked with him during the filming of *Major Barbara*; Constance Cummings and her husband, Benn Levy; Dame

Edith Evans, who starred in a number of Shaw's plays; Wee Georgie Wood and Arthur Askey I also owe a deep debt.

Others who helped me are Canon R J Davies, Rector of Ayot St Lawrence, where Shaw lived; Mrs Harold Thompson and her daughter, Mrs Rosemary Horton; Captain Lionel Ames; and Lady Lenanton (Carola Oman, the historian), who were Shaw's neighbours in the village; Dr T C Probyn, his doctor; Mr L W Plewes, his surgeon; and most of all Mrs Alice Laden, who was his housekeeper during the last eight years of his life.

Immense assistance and guidance were given me by Miss Barbara Smoker, whose knowledge of Shaw's life, based on her abundant records, is impressive; Mr Blair Maxwell, of R and R Clark of Edinburgh, who were Shaw's printers, and Mr Ian M Campbell, also of Edinburgh, for permission to quote from Dr William Maxwell's comments on Shaw's religious faith; Professor Dan H Laurence of New York University, who is editing Shaw's letters; John Stewart Collis; Maurice Collis, who sent me advance proofs of his biography, *Somerville and Ross* (Faber, 1968), containing Edith Somerville's diary entries commenting on Shaw's marriage; Alan Dent, who edited the correspondence between Shaw and Mrs Patrick Campbell (published by Victor Gollancz, 1952), and to the publishers and personal representatives of the late Mrs Cornwallis-West (professionally known as Mrs Patrick Campbell) for permission to quote from them; Leslie Johnson; Max Adrian, who in a two-hour solo performance on the stage impersonates GBS brilliantly; and Lord Evans of Hungershall.

A special word of thanks must be added to the British Broadcasting Corporation for allowing me access to their vast records library, where I was able to listen to many fascinating talks by Shaw and about him by well-known actors like Henry Ainley, Esme Percy, Beatrice Forbes Robertson and A E Matthews; and writers and friends, among them Lady Astor, Gilbert Murray, J B Priestley, A P Herbert, Sir Compton Mackenzie, C B Cochran and Sir Barry Jackson.

Index

219